WHAT BOOKS PRESS

AN IMPRINT OF

THE GLASS TABLE

COLLECTIVE

LOS ANGELES

WHAT FALLS AWAY IS ALWAYS

WRITERS OVER 60 ON WRITING & DEATH

WHAT FALLS AWAY IS ALWAYS

WRITERS OVER 60 ON WRITING & DEATH

KATHARINE HAAKE

EDITOR

GAIL WRONSKY

COEDITOR

WHAT
BOOKS
PRESS

LOS ANGELES

Library of Congress Cataloging-in-Publication Data

Names: Haake, Katharine, editor. | Wronsky, Gail, editor.
Title: What falls away is always : writers over 60 on writing & death /
    Katharine Haake, editor ; Gail Wronsky, coeditor.
Description: Los Angeles : What Books Press, [2021] | Summary: "Searing,
    poignant, and downright funny, What Falls Away Is Always brings together
    more than thirty writers of both prose and poetry to reflect on the
    experiences of aging and writing they share, along with the possibly
    more daunting question--what next?"-- Provided by publisher.
Identifiers: LCCN 2021023507 | ISBN 9781733378956 (paperback)
Subjects: LCSH: Authorship. | Aging. | Death.
Classification: LCC PN145 .W437 2021 | DDC 808.02--dc23
LC record available at https://lccn.loc.gov/2021023507

Cover art: Gronk, *Untitled*, mixed media on paper, 2021
Book design by Ash Good, www.ashgood.com

What Books Press
363 South Topanga Canyon Boulevard
Topanga, CA 90290

WHATBOOKSPRESS.COM

With special thanks to Rod Val Moore and Mona Houghton,
for their faithful counsel and enduring support;
to Gronk, as ever, for his boundless generosity and astonishing art;
to Aleida Rodriguez, for her invaluable contribution
in copy editing this book;
and to the Los Angeles Glass Table Collective
for starting it all.

In Memoriam

Katharine Sandholdt Haake, February 12, 1922—December 15, 2020
Richard Edward Haake, August 23, 1920—December 21, 2020

This shaking keeps me steady. I should know.
What falls away is always. And is near.
I wake to sleep, and take my waking slow.
I learn by going where I have to go.

— Theodore Roethke, "The Waking"

CONTENTS

RESPONSE

WHY YOU'RE SUCH
A GOOD POET

When you're writing a poem,
your courage shrinks until it is the
size of a comma. You have to
clamber up each of the letters with your
tiny feet, unable to see what lies
behind it. Each word plunges you
into an abyss. Last evening,
you wrote your name on the horizon,
right where the sun was setting, then
you lifted your pencil stub to the sky.
Only those who know that language
has no soul can drown in it. Only
the dead, who know the body has no
blood, just thin lines of graphite, can
make poems appear by erasing
everything you've written.

—Gail Wronsky

NOTHING TO DO

KATHARINE HAAKE

How difficult it would be, brother, to take leave of this earth.

—Christa Wolf, *Accident: A Day's News*

HOW DID WE GET SO OLD, so fast? a friend of mine recently asked.

Don't think it won't happen to you. You will get old; it will be fast.

That is, if you're lucky.

At a recent lovingkindness retreat, our monastic teacher spoke fondly of his grandmother when she was the age he likely is now. After a lifetime of hard work and virtue, she'd taken, he told us, to idling whole days on the porch, just sitting and rocking in her chair. Nothing to do, he described her with great tenderness, nothing to do.

Meantime, my 100-year-old father—still sound in both body and mind—complains of my 98-year-old mother, she just sits there all day, she doesn't *do* anything. They argue about the laundry; they argue about making the bed. I'm a woman of means, she grouses, but because her mind has gone as loose and porous as a sieve, she doesn't quite know what to grouse next. In all other respects, they are loving and kind to each other, but he misses the industrious wife he used to have.

I want to write: sometimes I pick up a pen and a piece of paper, but of course I just fire up my computer and rest my hands on the keyboard, where they have spent the better part of the last half-century. These days they lie there, unnaturally still.

Nothing to do. Nothing to do.

The story of how he became a monk, our teacher also told us, went something like this: he read a few books in high school, tried out meditation, traveled to what was once Burma, and then (he mused a bit wryly) somehow forty years passed.

In those same forty years, the writers in this book have also grown old. Along the way, it's safe to say, writing has remained the single most enduring constant of our lives. That much we share in common. But whether it serves to conjure the objects that release Katharine Coles into the "dreaming field of poetry," or to literally ward off death, as for Gary Young, each of us holds its gift with a separate part of our heart, knowing ourselves to be among the most fortunate people on earth because writing has helped trace the arc of our now long lives.

But it's not the same now as it once was, and not only because the late-stage artist looks back over many more years than lie ahead.

When Bret Lott reflects, for example, on what feels like a visceral need to tell stories, I remember that feeling with what amounts to an ache. *"We have to tell this story!"* But then, he allows, they never end up where we think they will. And even if that is, finally, the point, haven't we been doing this long enough? Except, of course, for that one last story that still needs to be told, and maybe, the next one after that.

We begin with desire as fierce and as strong as water. Now, we are rocks.

A memory: writing my first story on a beat-up couch in a weathered house one long college weekend in Santa Cruz. It was hot. The couch was brown and, like college couches everywhere, deeply soiled. Five years earlier, I'd read *Moby Dick* and stopped writing altogether; now I was taking it up again. Sentence by sentence, as Don DeLillo says, into the breach. Each one had to be right, to *sound* right. How did I even *know* to do that? I wrote all weekend, the last workshop story in my first creative writing class at the very end of college that grew to twenty pages and got me into Stanford. I haven't stopped since.

But I don't know. That's not quite true. There were those years when my sons were small and me just at the start of my academic career. There must have been lulls. Lately, it's been start and stop, sometimes more stop than not.

Still, more or less, a lifetime of writing.

"And this is all I have to show for it?" Patrick Bizzaro asks.

Looking back, it's clear: like Lott, I started out driven by the need to tell the story. Like Melanie Rae Thon, I believed—I still believe—that storytelling is "a human impulse, not a choice, but a necessity." That part hasn't changed.

But at some point, story slipped into writing and delivered me all-in to language itself. Which is to say, for years, I wrote the story out until one day it started writing me. In time, I would become all about only the making, pretty much the same as a clay pot or a meditation sit. I wrote because I wrote and because, I suppose, like Michael Ventura, that is "how I'm made," a little like breathing itself.

As my friend Sharman Russell and I like to say, you have to do something.

In her essay here, Russell contemplates how the making will continue into our dotage, when we find ourselves—as surely some of us will—well beyond even language. But for now, Sharman lives in a remote New Mexican river valley, although before COVID-19 shifted our lives into the ether, she used to come to LA twice a year to teach in the Antioch MFA program. When she was here, we'd take long, wandering walks on which we had long, equally wandering conversations about such eternal verities as ethics and writing.

Sharman is the author of nine books of science and nature writing and four speculative novels. Her nonfiction covers topics as diverse as butterflies, scientific pantheism, and childhood malnutrition in Malawi; her fiction transports and beguiles. Sometimes, on our walks, we talk about failure, a topic that never holds us long. But while it does, Sharman sometimes wonders what it might be like to have been better known or more widely read, while I suppose I would have liked to have been read or known at all. But soon enough, we circle back to writing, which in what once seemed like the vast expanse of our lives has always been central, the thing to ground and organize our days, to give them meaning. Not the meaning we were making, but the meaning *of* our making.

You have, after all, to do something.

In the spring of 2019, writers from the Glass Table Collective in Los Angeles presented a panel at the AWP conference in Portland in which we addressed the subject of this anthology—writing and death in what now counts as old age. We hadn't really expected to be there, writers on the way out who'd somehow slipped into both a city and a conference widely known for their celebration of youth. And since competition for panels is fierce but attendance can be sparse, we were also apprehensive. If no one showed up, we had plans for a drink.

Instead, we were dumbfounded by the buzz of interest in the SRO crowd that packed the large-sized conference room and greeted us warmly even before we'd begun, although in retrospect, this makes a kind of sense. Historically, we are part of the generation that entered the field when it was new and rode the tsunami of its explosive growth, coming of age as writers with the AWP itself. But not everyone, we noticed, in the audience was old. And as our nervousness gave way to the appreciative laughter, the murmuring assent that met our remarks, each of them, by turn, we began to wonder: what was this nerve we had touched? Later, others wondered too, which accounts for this book, the one you're holding now, where we have gathered other voices to consider what it means not just to have lived, but also to have written, for what is now a very long time.

Over the years, some of the things I wrote came true. None of them came true because I wrote them—that would be crazy to think. It's just in the nature of writing. But my most recent novel is called *The Time of Quarantine*, and while I didn't write the pandemic into being, the idea for a book on writing and death that took shape in Portland finds form in a world that's not the same as the world in which it was conceived.

"Once again," Christa Wolf writes in her post-Chernobyl novel, *Accident: A Day's News*, ". . . our age had created a Before and an After for ourselves" (36).

This time, not a nuclear threat but a viral one that, by virtue of state mandate and our own imminent mortality, had turned those of us in the "never grow old" generation into frail and elderly seniors overnight and seemed to be coming straight at us. Everything felt personal at first—age, a scary co-morbidity; our ruined travel plans, our wrecked retirements; grown children now unreachable in distant parts of the country.

Some of us thought like this. We were afraid.

In my case, safer at home means home alone. Could you get liquor delivered? My older son lives in Manhattan. Would we both end up strapped to a gurney in some overcrowded hospital corridor? I'd seen stuff like that on *ER* and *House*. It could happen.

But so far, it has not.

Not to me anyway, and not to those of us in this book, who remain among the privileged and will likely survive whatever history has in store for us again.

Still, writing in the present moment is tricky, and 2020 made it hard to keep up. We started this project wanting to explore what happens to writing as writers age and die, but in the context of pandemic and mass death, the passing of a single aging poet—even our own—is radically reframed. Only just last summer, as I began work on this introduction, we hadn't yet had the election that still lay in the future but is now in the past, the Capitol had not yet been breached, RBG was still breathing her last breaths on earth, the American West was burning all over again, Black lives were rising up—also again—and the benchmark of 200,000 remained unimaginable, never mind half a million. Whose lives matter, anyway? For of course, the genocide of climate change denial and systemic racism is utterly consistent with the political decision to let the virus "run its course" because the cure "can't be worse than the disease." Because, you know, in the pandemic, it's mostly dispensable people who die. Old people are going to die anyway. Old people are already almost dead.

Old people like us.

I'm just trying to make you remember what it was like in the heat of the crisis, during which a lot of the essays in this book were written. This is what Richard Katrovas calls "wet" knowing. And it is *hot*. Because even though we know we all come with expiration dates, when one day just last March we wake up and take in *it could be soon*, we realize, like Diane Seuss, that we don't really want to die.

None of this is what we meant when we gave our panel. Death was a provocative, if distant, conceit back then. Gail could write, with confidence, about late-stage writing; Chuck about losing his dog, his horse; Rod, the intimacy of writing that seeks to connect now more than to perform. We had our ideas. They were meaningful to us. They still are, only not in the same way.

In August 2020, I left Los Angeles for the first time in six months to make the seven-hour drive north to Sacramento to celebrate the occasion of my father's centennial birthday.

One week later, I turned 68.

Chronological age, my doctor once told me, is meaningless. We were in our 40s at the time, he and I, both healthy and fit, still almost immortal.

For many of us, growing old is such a slow process we hardly notice it. My parents, for example, did not admit to feeling it until sometime in their 90s;

my younger sister already laments it. Her knee creaks; she's tired: this is what it's like, she says, growing old.

As for me, it's hard to say. The present moment—the one we live inside—seems pretty much unchanged. Every morning, I wake to the same sun rising; the darkness of each night, the same. How, then, can I be old? Inside us all, the contours of the people we once were lie familiar and unchanging. I am still the girl who danced alone across the empty football field in a wild spring storm when I was in high school, the woman who rose daily to her writing desk as if it were the most natural place in the world for her.

My closest friend died at age 50; the man (not my former husband) whom I might call the true love of my life if we could still use words like that without self-consciousness or irony, at 56. If I live as long as my father, I will have lived twice as long as my friend, but oh, I do not wish to live twice as long as my lover.

Sharman's father-in-law, a retired colonel now 102, complains that you get to a point where life is just a long slog of outliving all the people you once knew and cared about. Who doesn't want to be the last one standing? But yet I never thought that it could last for half a century, the constant, unfathomable ache of loving the dead.

As a child, preternaturally attuned to the threat of nuclear annihilation, I did not expect to live to adulthood. Today, some sixty years later, apocalypse looks different but still threatens. Climate science tells us there will be winners and losers, but even though it's hard to see any winners just now, those of us in this book have already won. We won over and over and over, throughout our long years. Still living, still writing: what could be better? We lucked out.

In the early days of our quarantine, my heart stayed small, not wanting to lose yet. Nor did I turn instinctively to writing. Despite the sweet refuge of my canyon home, filled with objects I've collected over time and with its many windows looking out at trees and the California hillsides I have loved all my life, I found myself stunned, like the birds that fly into my glass and lie still on my deck, as if already dead.

Early in the summer of 2020, just when the pandemic was starting to surge here and we were finally taking in that we were in this for the long haul, I received an offer of publication for a book I have been working on for some years now, a memoir-in-essays that is, perhaps like Rod Moore's recent writing, among the most intimate things I have ever written, a long meditation on what I used to call loss but now recognize for what it is, which is death.

I was happy—a book! But when the offer fell through, I was oddly relieved. Still, the transaction triggered something. That old desire.

In *I Love Dick*, when Chris Kraus writes with excruciating detail about her need for recognition and the terrible taboo of saying so, the reader cringes. It's ok, these days, to talk about failure, but its corollary underside—desire for success—a kind of secret shame, especially at our age. What would people think? Better to be like the Argentinian writer Macedonio Fernández who spent forty years writing *The Museum of Eterna's Novel (The First Good Novel)* without any interest in publishing it. But maybe only up to a point.

Why are you still publishing? a student asks Christopher Buckley.

"Old writers," Aleida Rodríguez cites an unnamed online scrivener, "should move out of the way and make room for us."

Is there a quota? she wonders.

"Why give up your life?" Buckley asks. "Writing is largely who you are—no compelling reason to sit in a chair and just stare out the window or shop online." And he asks why the question of writing after 60 even comes up.

And so we ask, instead, what is writing to us now that we are old, and how has that changed over these many years we have been doing it?

For me, there's also this: the books I have written, both published and not: who was it that wrote them? Could that really have been me?

I've spent a couple of decades during my writing years when I was actively publishing and a couple of decades when I was not, but I've always been committed to the practice—and teaching—of writing as a primary experience, publication and all such other derivative effects being, as they are largely out of our control. But they are not nothing, and it's hard not to look back and assess what we've wrought—a sober reckoning. Even assuming the most modest level of discipline, just a few hours of work most weekdays, those of us gathered together in this book have collectively spent more than a million hours writing.

Gail says, why not? We're good at it, and we've had a lot of practice.

All of the writers in this book have grown deep and thoughtful with the insights of a lifetime. Most benefitted in their careers from when they came into the field. All are, by their date of birth, senior. Still, a lot of us would like to have had greater recognition.

But why do we want that, when the only real thing we can account for is the writing? We want this to matter. We want our lives to have mattered, as anyone would.

Because it is true, in the end, you have to do something.

And maybe doing something, if you bring your whole self to it, is enough.

Elsewhere, in an interview, Chris Kraus remarks that, in another life she might have been an activist, which she describes as a "true and worthy calling." But that's not what happened, she says; she became a writer instead (Friedman, 2017). By George, I thought, me too! For as a young woman in the turbulence of the Vietnam War era, I, too, wanted to be the kind of person who could charge out and change the world, and I, too, became a writer instead. The real question, Kraus continues, is who gets to speak. Yes, yes, I thought, the very question that has framed my own lifetime not just of writing, but also of teaching. You can make change in the world, and you can make it on the page, and while the two activities are not the same, they are also not unrelated.

The writers in this volume share an arc of history in which we all became writers, people for whom the act of writing has both a personal and a social value. And now we are old.

If, when you're young, you have the great good fortune to be taken up by something—long-distance running, guitar playing, woodworking, writing—you get to spend the rest of your life doing it, a life filled now with pleasure, meaning, and purpose because of the thing that has taken you up. But everything changes over time. When you are young, so much depends on just this sentence, just this word, just this story that must be—that *has* to be—told. The art of it all, the bearing of witness. Many years later, it takes a while even to notice that you have become the person who gets up every morning and spends a couple of hours with *The New York Times.* As the news grows grimmer, the hours slide by, until one day, the writing just stops. I say "you," when of course, I mean "me." But where did it go?

The feeling is deeply unsettling. If I'm not writing, who even am I?

The dying we imagined just a year or so ago, in the context of our writing lives, is also not the same as the dying the pandemic brought—and keeps bringing—all around us. It's hard to know quite how to feel about this.

Still, it's funny, what people can get used to. People can get used to a lot.

So maybe not today, or even the day after, but the day is coming when I will steel myself once more to the page, take a deep breath and begin, as ever, all over again. In fact, I have already done that by now: what I am writing is this. It will always be this, whatever "this" is in whichever moment. But I'm old enough now to know it won't last forever.

If sleep is a little bit like dying, when we ask a person in the morning, did you sleep well, are we really asking: did you die a little well?

When your parents live to be 100, 68 hardly feels old. A quick calculation and, why, you've got the whole span of your sons' lives, now men in the prime of their lives, to see what happens next. By the time you do, they'll be nearly old themselves. And isn't that a strange thing, your sons, old men, although I know they will never seem so to me.

But in some odd way I can't quite express, working on this book has aged me. In each of the essays, there it is again, as if it's been only a blink between the beloved childhood books we share with Mona Hougton—*When We Were Very Young* and *Harold and the Purple Crayon*—to this, our final chapter, *And Now We Are Old*.

Perhaps many more years still lie before him, or perhaps only a few," begins Jenny Erpenbeck's novel about a recently retired professor, *Go, Went, Gone*.

I breathe in.

When I entered my faculty early retirement program at the age of 67, I had to admit there wasn't anything "early" about it for me. The program allows me to continue half-time teaching for an additional five years, by the end of which I'll be 72, if I live that long.

I breathe out.

Let's do our best work in our 70s, Sharman exhorts me.

And yes, I think, yes. *Oh, let's*!

But then, finally, just as I was finishing work on this book, my parents did die—my mom, mercifully delivered from her plucky, late-stage dementia by COVID-19; my dad taken out by a bad fall five days later. They'd known each other all their lives and would soon have been married for three-quarters of a century, and I always said it would happen this way, that neither one of them could live without the other. After less than a week apart, my dad went to join my mother on the day of the 2020 winter equinox and the great Saturn–Jupiter conjunction, which seemed a poetic way for two such good lives to have ended.

As long as my parents held out, I remained, in ways both comforting and infantilizing, a child; death, an abstraction, reserved for others. And because I could not be there with them in their final months or hours, the sense of abstraction persists, but with a critical difference, as now, with the suddenness of all the things we know will come but still surprise when they do, I have become not just, at last, an orphan, but also, in the same breath, an old woman, a condition, I must say, I find extremely interesting.

"Every now and then," Nils Peterson quotes William Maxwell later on in these pages, "in my waking moments, and especially when I'm in the country, I stand and look hard at everything."

So here we stand, a bunch of old writers, looking hard at everything, more than a thousand years of writing among us. If you listen closely, you will find each voice that follows to be as true and constant as the stars they'll soon become.

Pressed, I don't suppose I know what earthly good it is, this practice I've devoted my whole life to. I don't even know what my brain is doing when I am doing it. There's a movement, I suppose, toward a kind of stillness, a bit like meditation, that has nothing at all to do with self but more the dissolution of self as it gives itself over to the act it performs.

In writing, what we want is closure. We want to find out what comes next.

But in life, the only thing we can know is what's already happened. Remember when, we say.

Remember when we left the mail to detox in the box?

Remember when we made all those masks out of old T-shirts and PJs?

Remember when we did not touch another human being for an entire year?

And wasn't that an odd time in the history of the world, we hope one day to say.

Because all at once, it happens, whatever is going to happen. I can't stop what's coming, and neither can writing. We started this book in a time of small things, and then the world shifted on its axis and things somehow got big, so the writing shifted too. Even the talks we presented in Portland are no longer the same, revised by their moment in history. Now, a new moment awaits as this book goes to press in the very moment we begin, each of us, to end our year of isolation and move back out into our strange, new world. But big or small, the essays in this book still hope to bear a kind of witness.

We live, we write, we die.

The monastic teacher at that meditation retreat whose grandmother sat and rocked on a porch is old now too. One day he told us about Jack Kornfield's teaching that when we get ready to die, most of us won't be thinking about how much money we made or fame we achieved or how many books we published, but will instead ask: did I love well? did I live fully? did I learn to let go?

Whenever I think about writing, there's an enormous sense of gratitude— I get to do this. And I also *got* to do this. I got to do it for years and years, fifty thousand hours of grace. How could anyone deserve so much?

And then we let go.

For each of the writers in this volume, the story of our writing as we approach the wall at the end of the world is unique. Only the wall is the same. And after we're gone, everything will be completely different, even as it remains exactly the same. Still, I wonder if we'll miss it, the writing. Maybe, we'll find, like John Cheever, or Alice Munro—or Andrew Merton's brilliant young MFA student who decided to stop writing and do something else with her one wild and precious life—that there's a sense of relief when the time comes to give up our long struggle with language, which in the end endures, and will endure, long after we do.

—*Los Angeles, January 2021*

WORKS CITED

Erpenbeck, Jenny. *Go, Went, Gone.* Translated by Susan Bernofsky, New Directions, 2017.

Kraus, Chris. *I Love Dick.* Semiotext(e), 1997.

————. "Who Gets to Speak and Why: A conversation with Chris Kraus. By Ann Friedman. *New York: The Cut,* June 2017, https://www.thecut.com/2017/06/chris-kraus-in-conversation-with-ann-friedman.html.

Wolf, Christa. *Accident: A Day's News.* Translated by Heike Schwarzbauer and Rick Takvorian, University of Chicago Press, 2001.

WHY THE DEAD
CANNOT ANSWER

A light, just now living, that has
never been, in its mortal life, turned off—

ON, it has never been, in its mortal
life, not ON,—

. . . when you ask what it is like

suddenly for what was always there
not to be there

for what had to be endured by those before you
to have to be endured now by you

LIKE, what in the world are such pervasive
vanishings LIKE,—

. . . no words it knows apply, and it is silent.

Silent. This is "the eternal silence of the dead."

—Frank Bidart

CALL

THE SENSE OF AN ENDING:
WRITERS OVER 60 TALK ABOUT DEATH

KATHARINE HAAKE

CHUCK ROSENTHAL

GAIL WRONSKY

ROD VAL MOORE

AWP CONFERENCE
MARCH 2019
PORTLAND, OREGON

IT WON'T BE LONG NOW

KATHARINE HAAKE

I DIDN'T START OFF THE IDEA of this panel thinking about aging but cut straight to the chase and called it death. You don't have to get old to die, but if you're lucky, you do. I'd just faced a health scare occasioned by potentially catastrophic lifelong effects of a congenital anomaly in my cervical spine I never knew I had that had left me recuperating for two months in a little, post-surgical nest of pillows on my window-facing couch looking out to the opposite ridge of my narrow canyon, largely immobile but not otherwise in much discomfort. I live alone. I had a lot of time to think.

In the book *Lives Other Than My Own*, which I read at the time, French writer Jean-Claude Carrière chronicles the experience of devastating loss in the lives of people to whom he is only tangentially connected—tsunami victims who take refuge in a Sri Lankan resort where he is vacationing; his girlfriend's sister, the mother of three young children, who is dying from cancer. "The first night you spend in the hospital, alone," he writes, "having just learned you are seriously ill and may die . . . is on the order of all-out war, a complete collapse, a total metamorphosis. It's a psychic destruction; it can be a re-foundation" (80).

In my case, no re-foundation, just a long, drawn-out period of tedium and reflection in which I conceived the idea of this panel.

Having lost two of the people closest to me when they were in their 50s,

I have also had a lot of time to mourn. They did not know each other and both died abruptly, after a brief struggle with different cancers of the blood, within a few years of each other. It won't be long now before the span of the time between my first friend's death and now will exceed the span of the time I once knew and loved her. My parents still live on their own in the house I grew up in; my father is 98, my mother, 96, although she sometimes self-reports as 102.

And there is also this: the discrete refusal of a one invited panelist, who politely declined. "There's so much discrimination against people over 60 in the arts," she wrote, "that it takes a certain sang-froid to come out under that banner," which, of course, I cited in our proposal justification and may well account for our being here.

I wasn't thinking about aging, either, when I made my way to my first mindfulness class in the fall of 2017. I was thinking about Trump. For nearly a decade, I'd been making excuses about not availing myself of classes offered by the nearby Mindfulness Awareness Research Center at UCLA, which somehow never fit into my schedule. Now, in the new political zeitgeist, I figured it was time to make my schedule fit to theirs.

The classes I have taken there have led me to many discoveries, one of which is me, an aging woman.

A new friend I met at MARC recently observed that a denial of death is also a denial of aging. She is 25.

In the absence of a dramatic re-foundation, I've been forced to reframe: Writers over 60 Contemplate Growing Old.

A recent *New York Times* article about a luxury retreat resort for elder tech workers, age 30 and up, begins: ". . . everyone was recovering from a long day sharing how hard it felt to be getting older. Some . . . walked pensively along the Pacific Coast at sunset. Others . . . browsed resort bookshelves, with sections labeled: 'What can death teach me about life?' and 'What are the unexpected pleasures of aging?'" Later, they'd "... paste stickers with ageist slurs all over their chests, arms and faces, and then hurl the stickers into a fire" (Bowles BU1). One 40-year-old "elder" lamented that, surrounded by people younger than he, the hardest thing was the loneliness.

Meantime, well past the age when my friends say of me, are you ever going to retire, and my students insist never, I, too, contemplate loneliness.

The recent Swedish novel *The Unit,* by Ninni Holmqvist, imagines a world where, at the ages of 50 (women) and 60 (men), "dispensable" people check themselves into a luxury research facility to serve as experimental subjects until they arrive at their "final donation," typically a set of vital organs but sometimes a toxic experiment. Dispensables are people who lack people who need them. If you don't have kids, you're out. Siblings don't count.

The recent Japanese novel *The Emissary,* by Yoko Tawada, portrays an environmentally degraded isolationist Japan where children ail and die in the care of preternaturally hale great-grandparents, of whom Tawada writes: "While it wasn't clear whether or not [they] would really have to live forever, for the time being they had definitely been robbed of death. Perhaps when their bodies had reached the end, even their fingers and toes worn down to nothing, their minds would hang on, refusing to shut down, writhing still inside immobile flesh" (93).

I'm not sure what all this has to do with writing.

The young wife of a famous poet many years her senior once confided in me that, for her, each decade had been better than the last. So far, that's been true for me as well. But even if, looking back, it's hard not to consider the body of writing that counts as at least part of what I have done with my life and think, is this all there is, the next thought is always, but what would I have done without it? I'm not so good at looking forward, but one day, if I'm lucky, I may wake to find myself, like my parents, very old, although, please not so old as Kane Tanaka, who, as the world's oldest human being at 116, might as well be a character in *The Emissary.*

Of course, it doesn't feel like that now. It just feels like any other old present moment, except this one is now. In the present moment, we breathe, we write. Until one day it comes to us as some big surprise: we can die, we will die, we do die.

As a child, I used to sit on rocks. I'd wander around the dirt lot at the far end of our school play yard just at the outer edges of town where the foothills stretched out and started to rise until I found the perfect boulder, and then I'd hunker down and settle into what I have only recently learned to recognize as the natural meditative state in which I spent much of my childhood. I carry this image in me always, a trace of the person just starting out still nested inside the layers and layers of me I have accumulated in the sixty years between then and now. Over those years, this—I don't know what to call it, sense of being? But not really, because it's as much an *absence* of being—would return to me at odd moments—hiking up a mountain trail, bathing my child, watching the light of the sun move across the water of the Gulf at my best friend's beach house shortly after she died. And I don't know—would it surprise me, or would I *recognize* it somehow? Would I turn as if to greet it—hello, my friend?

And then it would pass.

For the longest time, I arrived at this place, this rock, this breath—mostly through writing, for there's a moment in it when the letting go of thinking meaning hurls you out of the self as if in a kind of what Tim Meyers likens to ostension, what I call writing as a suture or a primary experience, and what my mindfulness teacher, Diana Winston, describes as "awareness of awareness." There's a certain headiness to this and, naturally, immense fragility.

As a girl, I sat on rocks. Later, I wrote.

These days, I'm learning, once more, to sit.

We used to believe that writing would heal us. It's not clear why we believed this. We believed it the same way we believed drinking orange juice for breakfast would improve our health or wearing comfort shoes would save us from bunions, neither of which turned out to be true. But let's be clear. By "we," I mean my dear friend Wendy Bishop, gone now for many years. She had her re-foundation, then, like the cancer victim in *Lives Other Than My Own*, she died.

The obituary of the second of my closest friends to die begins: "Gone Fishing."

So maybe after everything that's happened and all that we have done, it's fair to say that we were also right, and that writing healed us somehow, just not the way we thought.

WORKS CITED

Bowles, Nellie. "A New Luxury Retreat Caters to Elderly Workers in Tech (Ages 30 and Up)." *The New York Times*, 14 March 2019, p. BU1.

Carrère, Emmanuel. *Lives Other Than My Own*. Translated by Linda Coverdale, Picador, 2012.

Holmqvist, Ninni. *The Unit*. Translated by Marlaine Delargy, Penguin Random House, 2009.

Tawada, Yoko. *The Emissary*. Translated by Margaret Mitsutani, New Directions, 2018.

THE TUNNEL

CHUCK ROSENTHAL

I DON'T KNOW if I think about death more now than I ever did, though maybe now, at 67, I think about it differently and, often enough, think differently enough about it depending on what time of the day it is and who, particularly I'm thinking about.

Recently our dog died, and I feel her around me almost everywhere, in my house, on the property around it; what I feel is where she used to be, where she should be, though now she is irrevocably gone. I would like to believe that she has moved on somewhere, but there aren't many moments when I can make myself believe that, even though I often practice many things that I don't believe, just to feel what it would feel like to believe in them, say, a providential deity, or some pantheon of helpers between that great soul and we human souls, say Hindu gods, Catholic saints, Islamic angels, Hebrew messengers, Vajrayana sub-deities, maybe a paradise where great lovers share eternity; usually it doesn't change much of anything, and maybe I started to do this just before I turned 60, some nine or so years ago when I was 59 and diagnosed with cancer. It was then that I discovered that I was coward about death. Anyway, as you see, I'm not dead yet. Though now I know, undeniably, that I'm a coward about it, and often stalk my own life like a shadow, feeling myself in places that I don't occupy anymore, the tennis court, the top of a wave, the space above the rim. I'm more tentative about my plans five years from now, for ten years from now I have no plans.

Just before my mother, a devout Catholic, developed a glio brain tumor she told me she was ready to die. She was 55. She wasn't ready. Sad and disabled by her surgery, she suffered and died in about ten months. She was bitter. A mother of six, she never lived to see a grandchild. I had a camera then, a 35 mm. SLR. I took a photograph of her on her 55th birthday, developed it and printed it, tore it up and threw it out. I never took another. For her part, as my mother fell into her death, she abandoned many of her religious practices. What was the point? My mother's son, when I began my cancer treatments, I drank more booze. What was it going to do, kill me? I discovered Buddhism when I was twenty-one. I was pretty fervent then. I'm less fervent now. As the extinction of my *dukkha*, the end of my clinging to my precious selfhood becomes more inevitable, I've become less holy, more contrary. What am I doing with my time? What am I doing with this whiskey? Is someone (me?) enjoying it? Or not?

What am I afraid of? The unknown, I suppose. How much I'll miss myself when I'm gone. I'm less scared during the day when I'm busy, less scared when I'm drunk, more scared when I'm facing my cancer detecting blood tests that are coming up next week, most scared in the oneiric territory of the preconscious, in the morning, just before waking, when the reality and inevitability wash over me like bright light, when I fear my lover's death more frighteningly than my own, because then I might be waiting decrepit and alone. In those shivering moments I invite death. Bring it on, I say. But I don't know if I mean it.

I'm 67. Old enough to be wise. Where is my wisdom? Socrates didn't fear the nothingness. Neither did Buddha, who took comfort in the escape from the illusion of desire and pain. Whatever comfort Jesus took in the intimation that he might be the son of God, it didn't help him much that night in Gethsemane. When you throw suffering in with death things get really depressing. I try to think about late August on the Great Lakes when the leaves turned down and started to dry. The wind rattled them with the first whisper of winter and despite the warm and gentle days still ahead, I felt winter, white, cold, and dreadful in my bones. As horrible as some winters were, that fear was more visceral than in the actual winter, the winter, inevitably, that we got through. Maybe, maybe, it's like that.

As more people around me get sick and die, ones who meant a lot to me who I didn't even know, David Bowie, Leonard Cohen, others whom I knew, like Bill Gass, I gaze at those around me who are still alive, the still alive club. Do we congratulate ourselves? Whew, glad that didn't happen to me. Though I notice people my age trying to get healthier. What's the trick? Less meat? For the gift of long life and infirmity? If I hobble around at 67, what do I tell myself about the next ten years, do I quote my dying father, almost crippled to immobility? "I'll be playing golf in a week!" Things are going to get better? Do I clean up my past the way I'd clean the cat litter? Do I accept my life of hidden accomplishments? Do I line up my truths like duckpins? My failures? *Mea culpa*, not? Bleed optimism? Ooze despair? What do I got, a bad attitude? Okay, I should be happy I'll be dead before the really bad environmental shit comes down. Let the kids worry about it. I'm starting to think that I'm not the person who should be writing this essay.

I'm reading *The Magic Mountain*. Researching the siege of Vicksburg. Writing about a man lost in the sea of over-existence. Reading Bachelard, Whitehead, and Sartre. Suzuki. Always Shunryu Suzuki, the Zen Master whose last words were, "I don't want to die." On the commode, at the rate of a page a day, I'm re-reading Gass's *The Tunnel*. On my first reading, when I was in my 40s, I didn't get it. A tunnel out of house and home and life, past and future. Now I'm in there with him, digging.

ON LATE STYLE:
INTO ANOTHER INTENSITY

GAIL WRONSKY

THE "EAST COKER" section of T. S. Eliot's FOUR QUARTETS, his farewell to poetry, begins:

> In my beginning is my end. In succession
> Houses rise and fall, crumble, are extended,
> Are removed, destroyed, restored, or in their place
> Is an open field, or a factory, or a bypass.
> Old stone to new building, old timbers to new fires,
> Old fires to ashes, and ashes to the earth
> Which is already flesh, fur and feces,
> Bone of man and beast, cornstalk and leaf.

That seemed to me to be as good a place as any to begin thinking about what it means to be an older writer, to contemplate the end of a writing career. What is late style? When does it begin? What do writers generally do at the end of their lives, if they continue to write?

For starters, the concept of "lateness" is problematic because in most cases it can only be known retrospectively. Writers, particularly those who die young, can't know that they're writing their last work. But since this is a panel for "writers over 60," we can assume that it's time for many of us to start, or to have started, at least, thinking about late style.

So what do we do, we older writers, contemplating our last works, or books? Try to settle old scores, reach new heights, come up with a unifying theme, at last, or mount a last effort toward achieving some kind of purity of form? As a writer myself, just beginning to contemplate a late style, I'm horrified by those ideas! Part of me wants to be even more disruptive than ever—to break new ground, to subvert more expectations—my own and those of a reader. Part of me wants to find a pure style—purer than pure— purer than Wallace Stevens at his purest. To become pure language. Perhaps this is just a form of denial. A refusal to admit that age has happened, that death is coming.

Edward Said's last book, *On Late Style*, unfinished, is, appropriately, an examination of late style. What he says is that late artistic works (he writes about musicians as well as writers) are not always serene and transcendent meditations on eternity, or on the life lived, but on the contrary are quite often unresolved and contradictory—that they demonstrate a refusal to unite things which ultimately cannot be reconciled. He finds "fissures and fragments" in Beethoven; he discusses Cavafy's refusal to write about the present; he finds both "storminess and stillness" in Jean Genet. Overall, he finds a lot of "unsatisfied longing" allied to "cold detachment" in the late works of artists.

I find this fascinating—the sense that somehow, in the late work, there is an intersection between detachment and desire. Desire, the flame that feeds the work of young writers, doesn't disappear, isn't satisfied; one simply has some distance from it.

Shakespeare, the young man, writes *Romeo and Juliet*. The older man writes *The Tempest*, in which Miranda, the girl who has never seen anyone of her own human kind except for her father, exclaims, when she sees the shipwrecked crew, "Oh brave new world that has such people in it,"—to which Prospero, her father, replies, "tis new to thee." What's past is prologue; in my beginning is my end.

> So here I am . . . (writes Eliot),
> Trying to learn to use words, and every attempt
> Is a wholly new start, and a different kind of failure
> Because one has only learnt to get the better of words

For the thing one no longer has to say, or the way in which
One is no longer disposed to say it. And so each venture
Is a new beginning, a raid on the inarticulate
With shabby equipment always deteriorating
In the general mess of . . .
Undisciplined squads of emotion . . .

A raid on the inarticulate, with shabby equipment. Well, that sounds about right.

Eliot goes on in this poem to say, "Old men should be explorers," which is a phrase I've always puzzled over, even though I'm certain it's on a coffee mug in some catalog. Shouldn't old women be explorers? (Maybe he means both men and women, although I doubt it.) But why? Because when they get to a new place they won't find it new? Because they're going to die anyway so why not risk their lives? Because they'll be detached enough in their desires that they won't destroy what they find? Because they've seen it all already? I really don't know—it's one of those statements that appears, I think, to be more resonant than it is. Did Eliot consider himself an explorer? Or was that a wistful thought, a hopeless hope for something he knew he would never be?

He ends the poem with these lines:

We must be still and still moving
Into another intensity
For a further union, a deeper communion
Through the dark cold and the empty desolation,
The wave cry, the wind cry, the vast waters
Of the petrel and the porpoise. In my end is my beginning.

In my beginning is my end; in my end is my beginning. Does our late style re-evoke our early style? Did our early style predict our late style? It's something perhaps we writers over 60 should consider.

Here's a bit of a poem called "Death" that I wrote in my 20s:

Listen
To the gibberish of grief.
We cry and cry

A marble rooster stands
Beside the pool where eels
Are. Eyes
Like rhinestones boiling in blue ink.
His sheets   I ironed them.
His coffin   I drew then named.
The silver leaves of ash
Catch what the soul sheds:
The moonlit, inarticulate waste.

And these lines from a more recent poem:

So much said already in the twilight
We are alive, but do not demand much of it

We don't believe in anything but ghosts
We don't question people badly dressed in mourning
Under the heavy heel, we are alive and weightless
Under the capsized boat we fly.

My end in my beginning? My beginning in my end?

Clearly, early on, I was more infatuated with surrealism, with notions of glamour, than I am now. I seem more resigned, now, less infatuated with the whole notion of dying, but still committed to finding a bit of magic in the life being lived.

Today all of my writing strikes me as movement toward "another intensity," albeit with the same old shabby equipment. Tomorrow? Fissures and fragments, storminess and stillness, I feel it coming on.

O BODY SWAYED TO MUSIC

ROD VAL MOORE

SOME OF YOU MAY HAVE HEARD this story about Anthony Burgess—how a doctor told him that he had only a year to live, and that this terrible news prompted Burgess to hurriedly write and publish three or four new novels in the space of that year. When I first heard that (possibly apocryphal) anecdote many years ago, I said to myself, *Oh yes, that's what I would do too*. At the very least I'd undertake to challenge as best I could the utterly unacceptable idea of dying "before my pen has gleaned my teeming brain," as per Keats.

However, in the course of time, in the course of reaching my late 60s, my feelings about that have evolved somewhat. While the doctors have not given me a year to live, Nature, bloody Nature, has given me the admittedly less dire but still unbelievable news that I have, let's say, twenty years to live, give or take a decade (or two). But no, I cannot react to this strong sense of an ending as I might have long ago. Of course, I do, like everyone my age, feel time right there at my back, in the form of a chariot, a gun barrel, or a parade of the ghosts of loved ones who have already left this world.

But in fact, that death sentence, as it were, does not inspire in me a desperate urge to unleash a flood of fiction and/or poetry. I am definitely not moved to try too terribly hard to achieve a much wider audience, to aim for something along the lines of literary fame. Like a percentage of others my age, authors and other cultural workers alike, I find myself moving certain degrees of distance from the passion of my earlier years, immersing myself more in attitudes of reception than production, opening myself more to philosophy, spiritual mutterings, surrendering myself more to wisdom than offering myself as a wise man.

None of this is to say that I abandon the practice of writing. Far from it. What I do abandon, cheerfully is a certainty that was once deeply embedded in my bones, that the craft of language is my truest and best means of fulfillment. Now, and maybe this is familiar to some of you, I also find fulfillment in the absence of writing. I find it in exercising my duty to exist, to maybe lyrically and simply exist, to craft a living presence that is partly informed by the degree of self-reflection that writing has gifted me, and partly informed by the quality of interaction with those I love.

When in fact I am writing (something, by the way, I still do every day), I approach the page with a narrower set of expectations. My fiction and poetry still engage, of course, in some form of brain gratification, some brain gleaning, but they have also shifted from the internal toward the external, in that they can function more deeply than they used to as *gifts*, as heartfelt gestures of love and friendship. Whitman, in *Leaves of Grass*, explains how, at his death, he thinks of leaving behind no "literary success nor intellect, nor book for the bookshelf, / But a few carols vibrating through the air... / For comrades and lovers." Lewis Hyde, in his chapter on Whitman in *The Gift*, reads parts of *Leaves of Grass* as explorations of the idea of death itself having a gift value, how it takes on the increased value as a result of dispersal, just as in Whitman's promised transubstantiation of corpse into grass, and that our books—or if not books, our interactions—might be seen, once we are gone, as beautiful, abandoned forms with potential for adoption as differently beautiful forms.

At any rate, these are only some of the actions and attitudes I find myself developing these days in my jolly and not so jolly conversations with death. I have *not* yet reached the stage that Prospero foresees in Act 5 of *The Tempest*, when he says that "every third thought" will be . . . his grave. Maybe, in my case, every three thousandth thought? Whatever the number, it's not the tomb and the worms that come to mind but . . . simply . . . the sheer absence of being . . . or even the dear absence of being. In one of my favorite

Auden poems, a grim voice with a dark message drifts among the suicidal: "The earth is an oyster with nothing inside it, / Not to be born is the best for man." A dismaying notion indeed, though persuasive to many of us at times, if I'm not mistaken. But, happily, the poet goes on: "The second best," he says, "is a formal order." Here my writer's mind brightens a bit. *Oh, he's right*, I can claim. That's me, that's what I do. I take the raw materials of the culture, the discourse, the intellect, and what do I do? I formalize. I apply cohesion and coherence!

Here are those final lines of Auden's poem, "Death's Echo."

> The desires of the heart are as crooked as corkscrews,
> Not to be born is the best for man;
> The second-best is a formal order,
> The dance's pattern; dance while you can.
> Dance, dance, for the figure is easy,
> The tune is catching and will not stop;
> Dance till the stars come down from the rafters;
> Dance, dance, dance till you drop.

That's it! I thought, upon a recent re-reading. The secret lies somewhere in the idea of dancing. The writer is the dancer, the book the dance. And I will dance while I can!

Or not. As a teacher of writing for many years, I did my best to persuade my students that writing is NOT a dance, not a performance at any rate, at least not in the way they tended to think of it. How burdensome a chore it was for some of them to put sentences down on the famous blank page when they imagined every word a kind of misstep in a dance, a sour note in a recital, each error noted by their dancing master, who watched frowningly, slapping his staff against his palm, just offstage. No, no, I would tell them. Writing may come easier if you approach it as a conversation with one or two friends or relatives. Think of it as a long Facebook comment, I told them, or something like that, at least in order to get yourself started.

But in fact, now that I no longer have to worry about 20-year-olds and their writing fears, I have come to view my own process, especially as my drafts develop, as, yes, a kind of dance, and therefore I come now to the point where I will combine my ideas into a:

Dance Macabre Manifesto *(With special thanks to Lucia Ortiz Monasterio)*

1. Forget all previous dancing. For example, forget the time you were in the junior high auditorium, doing the jerk, and the one you were supposed to be dancing with turned to her friend in order to point at you and laugh.
2. Find other ways, maybe gifts of writing, to please lovers and comrades.
3. Take advantage of superannuation's famous erosion of the super ego, to renew your enjoyment of expressive dancing, but making sure to sometimes dance alone just as you write alone.
4. Dance and dialog must inspire thought, inspire writing. It is said that Socrates took up the art of ecstatic solo dancing at age 70. A year later he died without fear.
5. Walt Whitman states that "thinking wants to be learned as . . . a kind of dancing." I say let the writer's mind imitate the lonely dancing body in its refusal of intent, refusal of shame, refusal (despite Auden) of formality.
6. Meanwhile, it's pointless to write too much about dancing per se. Better to incorporate the lessons of dance into the writing, playing with notions like surprise, lightness, explosion, geekiness, while avoiding more obvious dimensions such as tempo or pattern.
7. Listen to an hour of dissonant music, then turn it off and proceed to construct similar melodies in your head. Write just below the surface of that pure inventiveness, finding the language that exists there and giving it [so hard to avoid!] some degree of cohesion.
8. When dancing, dance as if you are stomping on music's grave, moving your feet out of sync with the tune that keeps playing. Then dance over to fiction and/or poetry's grave, and do likewise.
9. Imagine all four of your limbs as semaphores that spell out the details of forests as well as cities as well as deserts. Then remember that meaning is always breaking. Remember that the glass is already broken.
10. Nietzsche said that he couldn't believe in a god who doesn't dance. Be a god who dances, then put that kind of dance into words.

SOURCES OF INSPIRATION

W.H. Auden, "Death's Echo"

Lewis Hyde, *The Gift: Creativity and the Artist in the Modern World*

John Keats, "When I Have Fears That I May Cease to Be"

Lucia Ortiz Monasterio, "Wonderful Advice from Socrates and Nietzsche: Dance, Dance Alone"

Shakespeare, *The Tempest*

Walt Whitman, "No Labor-Saving Machine"

Portland, March 2019

———

Not so long after that, everything changed.

RESPONSE

FEAR OF FALLING

watching oneself, a writer's predilection or handicap is seemingly.
in my best judgment on the upswing. those things below are steps.
that in part. and curbs. but also the operations of recall, much worse,
perhaps self-conscious. still the pestle was, despite effort, without the mortar.
the murmur still murmur and not bees. pieces of what once was called
bodyparts unruly, knees, surgeries, nerves activated highly, then caput.
think falling a long way. first as a child, now worse. morose.
imagine an act executed in the present and no way to witness its arc.
events ever receding. some hyper and unrecalcitrant off-switch.
watch the proceedings. a picture 530 feet above the streets of Calgary
online. never been. hypothetical stalks. world. snow. wind is wind.
wispy thinning knotting wind. get-it-done ticking. worn mostly out.
can't what is. take it in. dress it in. dizziness & vortexes. undoings.

—Martha Ronk

I DON'T WANT TO DIE

DIANE SEUSS

THIS LITTLE ESSAY was going to be one way. Now it has to be another way. It pisses me off that its direction was waylaid by a fucking pandemic. That last sentence was meant to sound as stupid and self-absorbed as the average American. The first version of this essay on writing after age sixty was going to sound wise. This version will sound stupid. I could be semi-wise about writing toward death when death was not a looming reality. Now I'm wiping down my mail with bleach.

I spent my whole life writing about death. All along I guess I should have been writing about life but writing about death was how I wrote about life. I learned young that death is an artificial boundary. I had an ongoing relationship with my father, who died when I was seven, and as others fell on their swords or paring knives, I had relationships with them too. Maybe that's what the imagination is for. How wrong I was. Death is not an artificial boundary. It's as dumb and real as Trump's wall. It's as dumb and real as artificial flowers. It means no more TV. No more memory. No more weather and bitching about the weather.

All of my favorite writers speak to and from the dead. Now, now that I'm facing the fact of it, I'm not sure I want anyone talking to or from me. I'm not sure my corpse will be happy about that. Anyway, what good will it do me?

I'll still be dead. A stiff. Cadaver. Carrion (Hopkins). Dead. "(T)he dog won't have to / sleep on his potatoes / any more to keep them / from freezing" (Williams). At least Plath got to rise out of the ash with her red hair and eat men like air. At least Plath got her own particular oven, her own pile of ash. I want to live to dye my hair red again. Today the United States Centers for Disease Control and Prevention recommended live-streaming funeral services to cut down on exposure to the virus.

Unless they are over eighty-five, or queer, or Black, or Native American, or Middle Eastern American, or Asian American, or Jewish, or Latinx, or poor, or homeless, or addicted, Americans don't have the capacity to imagine mass casualties of people like themselves. I'm afraid of Americans (Reznor, Bowie, me). We (white Americans) are selfish and ignorant. Most are not following social distancing orders. Students with faces the color of uncooked pie dough say they deserve their spring break in Florida and they're gonna take it. People who don't watch the news or watch the wrong news crowd the dollar stores, loading up on stuff. They deserve their stuff and they're gonna take it. On the other end of the stepladder, where narcissism collides with opportunism and makes a baby, Trump wants to reopen the economy. What's a few million lives shaved off the bottom. The old, the infirm, the poor. Two birds, one stone. "Our country wasn't built to be shut down" (Trump). We built this city on rock and roll (Starship). (Rolling Stone poll winner, Worst Song of the eighties).

My mom, age 90, is doing it her way. She's conserving food and energy. Making soup with what's left in the crisper. Where I'm from we call that garbage soup. She's remembering odd details about her long life. Today, on a phone call, she told me that out of the blue she remembered a man named Ford French who liked burned toast. A sparrow has taken up residence in her window feeder. It just sits there, watching her TV through the picture window. My brother-in-law, disabled from the aftereffects of Agent Orange in Vietnam, has been getting back in touch with hometown friends who, like him, went to war. One, Dave, who lives in a shack in the upper lower, told Dewey he bought 100 cans of sardines, a sack of dried beans, and 50 packages of Orville Redenbacher popcorn. He's catching and eating carp from the river. He fell off a ladder and broke both heels. Made his own casts from an old exercise mat.

Back when I was wise, I had a whole diatribe to lay out about writing toward an ending. It had crocuses in it, and snowdrops. Being from rural Michigan I know the names of flowers. My diatribe was also a bit bitchy about the state of contemporary American poetry. The marketing angle. The crowdsourcing. The hairdos and eyebrows. The celebrity. The social media posts by young poets saying, "Fuck Keats. Fuck Shakespeare." One more round of *make it new*. How tedious that essay would have been. How mean-spirited. Witchy. Not a cool, green, voluminous witch, but a dried-up hag of a witch who doesn't want to be replaced. Who fears a mass grave. Not just filled with bodies but with poems judged passé by the young. This is no country for old (wo)men (Yeats, me).

I just walked my dog through the small campus where I was once young. It's a ghost-campus now. The children have been sent home to wait out the plague. It's easy, given the emptiness and fog, to see myself as I was then, peyote-tripping with my roommate, wearing a shower curtain for a cape, spouting witticisms. "Fuck Melville. Fuck Emerson. Fuck Wallace Stevens. Fuck Marianne Moore with her tri-corner hat." What obnoxious assholes we were. How we would have taken to Instagram culture if it had existed then.

Our "fuck this" and "fuck that" plus forty years of dues-paying got us where we are today. On the doorstep of a plague. My roommate. Me. Our generation, now the focus of derision. Well, we deserve it. So do they—the young, stripping our gingerbread houses of sugar. Inside, apron tied around my thick waist, I'm lighting the logs in the walk-in oven.

My fear has exposed the hollowness of what I thought I knew. Now I want to live (Susan Hayward). I want to watch *The Price Is Right* and cry when some dumb fuck wins a stainless steel refrigerator. I want to touch people. I want to see my mother again. My sister. My son. I want to write an epic, a postplague epic about American ignorance. I'm afraid of Americans (Bowie). I don't give a damn 'bout my reputation (Joan Jett). Reunited and it feels so good (Peaches and Herb). I want to move home. Take me to the river, dip me in the water (Al Green). I don't want to die (Freddie Mercury). (Me).

"I Don't Want to Die" first appeared in *Lit Hub*, March 25, 2020.

THE HEART BREAKS, AND BREAKS OPEN: SEVEN REASONS TO TELL A STORY THROUGH ALL AND EVER:

MELANIE RAE THON

1.

Last Sunday, the beautiful woman on TV, the soldier home from Iraq with shrapnel still deep in her brain, said doctors gave her one chance in a hundred to wake, one in a thousand to do more than bob and babble. And here she was, radiantly amazed, smiling sweetly.

Somebody had to be the one, she said. *Why couldn't I do it?*

In a tent, in a field hospital outside Baghdad, Jodee Beddia's surgeon cut a piece of bone from her skull so her swelling brain wouldn't kill her. *Sewed it inside my abdomen*, she said. *To keep the bone alive.* So nobody would lose it. Jodee Beddia flew home in a coma.

Now the bone is back in her head—she's stapled and sutured. *Pain, yes, always. Like light*, she says, *cutting through me.* She traces a line from between her eyes, up over the crown, through both temples. She smiles. *It's only pain, a friend if you call it that, not so bad to be awake, alive today to feel it.*

2.

The chickadee comes to the feeder. Even now, so close to twilight! Less than half an ounce of feather and hollow bone, ten drops of blood, heart smaller than a fingernail—yet she survives all night, every night, all winter.

3.

One bright day last fall, thirteen-year-old Rosanna Rios arrived at the hospital in time to give her heart and lungs—liver, spleen, pancreas, kidneys. In time to surrender her perfectly clear corneas and twenty-six inches of unscarred skin to save the lives, restore the sight, heal the burns of seven others.

Why should a 69-year-old man receive the heart of a child?

4.

Rescuers find one bruised baby in a field of tall grass, alive and unafraid after a tornado, this one of nine hundred lifted up and set down, everything destroyed around her.

5.

The tanager swoops tree to tree, gold and orange, black-winged, silent. Frogs chirp at dusk, and swallows dive, catching insects. Everything loves life: bird, child, fish, mosquito—you hear the fluttery *whoosh* of your own heart:

Let your body rise.
Let the wind blow through you.

You will die. But not tonight. Tonight, the whole world is here alive inside you, everything you've loved and lost: the white horse haloed in morning light; your child; your father; violet pansies blooming under snow, the ones you found in your mother's garden.

The thrush hidden in the woods holds one shimmering note so bright and clear you think the bird will shatter—and then it does shatter: into a heart-sparking ripple of song that splits down your bones and bursts from your body.

You speak now because you too are shattered, because the heart breaks, and breaks open. The people whose stories you hear, the miraculous beings you encounter, have fallen inside, and now, before you die, you hope to learn to love them. Imagining their lives is the path you walk to do this.

6.

I believe storytelling is a human impulse, not a choice, but a necessity. Unlike the old idea that memories are "wired" in the brain, synapses seared for (almost) all time, current research indicates that "reactivating a memory destabilizes it, putting it back into a flexible, vulnerable state."

In other words, every time you remember an episode of your life, you are reinventing it: embellishing, deleting, altering it through fusion and imagination.

If you cannot imagine, you cannot remember.

There is no such thing as "I."

Re-*membering* is transformation!

Every person on this earth is a storyteller.

Our memories are shifting collages, narratives spun from fragments, ceaseless prayers, explosions of sensory impressions, webs so splendidly complicated we have no hope of translating experience into language.

Yet we persist in trying to do so.

Every living being, human and more-than-human, is an infinite mystery.

Every moment of love is filled with the love of a lifetime.

7.

Now, as I speak, some memory has come back to you. Now, in your own mind, you are inventing a story.

In *Camera Lucida,* Roland Barthes described the *studium* and *punctum* of a photograph. There are elements of composition and subject matter the photographer chooses consciously or deliberately. This is the *studium.*

And there are elements that pierce the frame by chance. For instance, the photographer is "shooting" Nicaraguan soldiers, and two nuns pass by in the background. This is the *punctum,* the unplanned, unchoreographed moment the photographer sees (gasping, no doubt, in wonder) and records. Barthes says the "adventure" of this photograph comes from the co-presence of these disparate elements.

Now, as you enter the adventure of your own memories, leave space for the unplanned, the unexpected, the piercing impressions that shatter the frames of individual lives.

Every story offers you the possibility of transcendence, the opportunity to imagine, to love the ones who have stepped into your frame and forever altered your experience.

We speak because we will die; but while we breathe on this earth, every moment is eternal.

SOURCES OF INSPIRATION

"Out of the Past," by Kathleen McGowan, *The Best Science and Nature Writing 2010.*
Camera Lucida, by Roland Barthes.
Mother Teresa: *Lord, let my heart break open wide enough for the whole world to fall inside.*
"The Red Poppy," by Louise Glück, in *The Wild Iris.*

EVERYONE OF A CERTAIN AGE

KIM ADDONIZIO

I MADE IT TO 27 before my first truly personal, knowledge-entering-the-marrow encounter with death. Not that I'd been entirely untouched: there had been the next-door girl with polio, whose house I was frequently brought to as a companion and playmate. Eileen was her name. I don't remember that we did much but sit awkwardly in her living room, she in her wheelchair and me on the edge of the couch, with Kool-Aid and cookies. She was fourteen, and I was seven. The braces on her legs, the wild gestures of her hands, her voice—it resembled a stroke victim's, a slow garble of wide-open vowels, hard to decipher—and whether this was from the polio, or whether my memory is faulty and it was something else that had pressed down too hard on her brain or body—all this made me anxious and resentful, longing to get out of that gloomy, doomed house and back to my sunny front yard. One day my parents told me she had died. I don't remember any feeling being attached to the news; if there was, it was probably relief.

In junior high there was a boy I knew, a little, who put his father's shotgun in his mouth. This was harder to absorb, mostly because the idea of suicide was so foreign. Who would want to end their life, and why? I would understand this impulse much better later. He was a grade behind me, and I knew his older brother a little, too, and mostly I felt sorry for the brother left alive. In high school, a girl I only knew by sight, one of the popular crowd, was killed by a falling tree while she was driving. Her little brother, in a child's car seat next to her, was unharmed. It was that fact that really stayed with me, the capriciousness of it.

These deaths were aberrations in the pattern of my life. Edna St. Vincent Millay wrote, "Childhood is the kingdom where nobody dies," and I assume it was true for her, as it was nearly true for me. Other kids, of course, aren't so lucky. It's assumed that the natural order of things is innocence and gradual knowledge for children, and eventually growing old, but that's not an assumption that holds up for long. Children lose people, and children, too, die. Sometimes in great numbers, through war and famine. We know that, but the universe feels particularly cruel, or indifferent, when some lives end before they've barely begun. It feels viscerally, fundamentally unfair, and it is. To be a parent and imagine losing your child is a particular vision of a hell you hope never to descend into. I once had a dream that my daughter, an actress in her thirties, skipped onstage for a part, lost her footing, and fell over the edge of the stage. I was behind her and rushed to the edge to see her lying on concrete, blood pooling around her head. I knew she was dead, and my immediate thought was: *My life is over.* I knew, in the dream, that I would have to kill myself. I'm pretty sure that's how I'd feel in waking life, too.

But my real, deeply felt losses have been the predictable ones, the ones we call normal. Expected, generational losses. Growing up, all but one of my grandparents were dead or absent already, so it was my father's death that first knocked me down. Though I understood by now that death was actually part of the pattern of life, rather than the breaking of it, that knowledge did nothing to ease my grief. The deeper knowledge was simply this: he was gone. I'd never seen a corpse, and when I saw his I knew that whoever, whatever, had once animated my father had vanished. The hole in the world where he had been would not be filled.

It took a few years for the next deaths to occur, and for the next realization to sink in: the older I got, the more of those irrevocable losses I was likely to experience. And that, as the saying goes, is the good news. The alternative was that I wouldn't be around to feel them.

My grandmother, who had lived with us most of my life and stayed with my mother in my parents' house after my father's death, took an overdose of sleeping pills at 92. My mother made it to about the same age, after years of decline from Parkinson's. I was in my 50s by then, and my friends were watching their own parents go down, none of them gracefully. The concept of aging gracefully strikes me as tenable only up to a certain age, after which it strikes me as bullshit. Buddhists seem to have a better handle on this, with their acknowledgment of impermanence, the declining and dying body all part of the process. Certain cultures—Native American and Chinese come to mind—traditionally revere the wisdom of elders. But as everyone of a certain age understands, it's not easy to grow old in a culture that isn't much interested in what you know. Your hard-won wisdom, if you've managed to attain any, is irrelevant. You begin to grow transparent, invisible to the young on the streets, eventually to disappear, often into a warehouse for others of your kind, and then altogether.

The facility in which my mother spent her depressed, deteriorating final years, repeating her mantra—*I've had a good life, I'm just waiting to die*— required a series of attitude adjustments for the unwary visitor. It resembled a Marriott in the well-appointed lobby, but the dining room was more like a Holiday Inn, and her small, dim room was like a budget motel you wanted to check for bedbugs, cobwebs, possible mold in the bathroom. A few months after she died, one of my brothers, a year older than I, succumbed to the liver problems that had plagued him after a transplant. I was approaching the time of life at which greater numbers of people are felled by cancer, strokes, heart attacks. This, too, was normal, part of the pattern.

At 65, I can feel my corporeal presence beginning, just slightly, to attenuate. It's as if, day by day, I'm displacing a smaller volume of air. I've spent my life trusting in the strength of my body, and it's only in the past year that I've begun to see signs of diminishment. First there were the floaters in my eyes, accompanied by little electrical flashes. This, it turned out, was something called Posterior Vitreous Detachment. My doctor assured me it wasn't uncommon for aging eyes. A few months later, a series of routine blood tests showed alarming amounts of certain enzymes in my liver. Had years of drinking caught up with me? As it turned out, no. The enzymes had spiked because, in order to cope with two weeks of painful back spasms, I'd been overdoing the alcohol in combination with an herb called kratom. The liver values settled down after a couple of weeks, and I made an appointment for a bone density test, convinced I would sail through, but again, no: despite regular cardio-weight workouts and yoga, I had osteopenia, next door to osteoporosis.

Then, shortly after COVID-19 blew into town, I came down with shingles. "Normal for older people," my doctor, in her thirties, once again assured me. I understood: my immune system wasn't what it used to be.

COVID has become the inescapable subject for all of us as I write this, in late April of 2020. Possibly this is a darker account because of the pandemic, death occupying more space in my head. I'm now part of the "vulnerable population." As a senior—not a word I particularly want to embrace—I'm eligible to go to the grocery store during certain hours set aside for older citizens. I'm also considered expendable by a number of people who overtly or privately consider that this disease may be a less-than-unwelcome culling of the herd. AIDS, as "the gay plague," was ignored for years by the powers-that-be while all around me, in 1980s San Francisco, were skeletal young men being pushed in wheelchairs or carried into hospital emergency rooms by their lovers. Now, COVID is disproportionately killing the old, the poor, prisoners, African Americans, the medically compromised. You know that, and you know the rest—the daily headlines and news articles, the dire economic figures, the highlighting of class and racial injustice, the bungled response of this self-serving administration, our collective fears and moments of grace. The pattern of all of our lives is being broken, or remade, or maybe after all simply being revealed once more: uncertainty governs us. Change is the mad, capricious ruler of this kingdom, and we are all its subjects.

My younger brother recently sent me a scanned newspaper photo of our mother, who was a champion tennis player, serving for a match. It's May, 1945, a sunny day in Palm Springs, California. A crowd sits on risers in front of a low building with a tile roof, palm trees rising behind it. My mother is up on the ball of her left foot, pivoting on her right, her wooden racket poised behind her head. The ball floats in the air above her, ready to be slammed across the net. At this moment, anything seems possible; an ace, a fault called, a perfectly placed shot that engenders a swift rally or a long exchange.

She's going to win, defeating her opponent in three sets, 6-0, 2-6, 6-4. It occurs to me that for all the vagaries of memory, the past is the only thing that is truly certain. Part of me wants that ball, that tiny white sunlit orb, never to come down. I know it will. I know I'll be born, that I'll become a writer, that she'll be miserable for the final years of her life and that one day I'll sit with her after feeding her a single chili bean, watching her attempt to sign her name. I don't know what my own fate will be, whether I'll be undone by a reckless driver, or catch COVID and start coughing and die alone and intubated, my last breaths overseen by a stranger in a mask and gown. Whether I'll find myself in the kind of place my mother ended up, or have a series of strokes like my father, or a failing liver like my brother. Maybe my daughter will be there, wherever "there" is, and there will be music I love and enough morphine. There are endless possibilities to consider what will make an end of me.

I've found it harder to write as I've grown older, as so much of my thinking and experience has already found its way into books of poetry and fiction and memoir. I've wondered what I have left to say, and whether it's of any value. Now, in the midst of a global pandemic, I feel both smaller and enlarged, moved by so many stories of what it's been like for other people. I can't know what's coming, but I know this: each of those stories is important. No one is expendable.

There is a great silence on the other side of the present moment. And while we are here, we must make what noise we can. In crowded cities, people are leaning out their windows or standing on their stoops or fire escapes and clapping. In Italy and elsewhere, they sing. In my Oakland hills neighborhood, in the woods above a canyon, people have taken to howling at 8 p.m. Coyote yips, wolf cries, dog barks, and the actual dogs, happily or mournfully, joining in. Little kids, delighted, yell as loud as they can. Once I got out my tambourine and set up a rhythm, and somewhere there was an answering rhythm, pounded out on a deck railing. This collective raising of voices happens every night. Then the sounds slacken to a little wind stirring the leaves, occasional bird calls. The howling of my neighbors lasts only a minute or two. We can't see each other, and I've never met any of them, but it heartens me to hear them.

THE GREAT ERASURE

JOY MANESIOTIS

*The struggle to find a poetry in which your survival rather than your defeat
is celebrated . . . to at least find a way to survive amidst an ethos that
relishes your erasures and failures is work that . . . women have to do.*

—Rebecca Solnit, *Recollections of My Nonexistence*

WHEN I FINALLY looked at my phone, the list of alerts—texts and
phone calls from my friend— streamed down its face. I hadn't been touching
my phone because I was in the small grocery store in a small town on the
Oregon coast. I was wearing a mask. As was almost everyone else. Almost.
Okay, this is a common story now.

A friend had been staying in my house in California. A spark arcing to the
lights on top of the kitchen cabinet, and ignition, the cabinet in flames: the
kitchen on fire.

———

I had wanted this essay to be about invisibility. About being erased. About
being erased while still here on earth, a woman in her sixties, almost invisible
in our culture. Almost invisible in the literary world. I thought that was what I
was going to write.

———

I had wanted to say: I laugh in the face of death.

———

The Fates were older women, clearly past 60. Who spun the threads of destiny, with absolute power over the universe: *Clothos* (Spinner); *Lachesis* (Alloter); *Atropos* (Unalterable): Μοιραι: the goddesses who distribute, meting out the events of our lives. *Atropos*, who has the most decisive agency, who renders all other actions immutable. She cuts the thread.

———

Smoke, thousands of particles of soot, filling the room, sucked through the AC system, my friend ran outside, and while she waited for the emergency crews, the fire sprinklers came on inside the house—one sprinkler, pumping thirty to fifty gallons of water per minute, spinning into the soot and smoke and flinging it in arcing circles over the kitchen and family room, the cabinets filling with water, the wood floors soaking it in, the stainless steel range a kind of oversized bucket.

———

So, why keep writing? Perhaps the act is not about being heard or maybe not even about speaking, at all.

———

I had so easily reached for cumin, opening the drawer with spices stacked in my partner's ingenious design—that small *frisson* of pleasure. The satisfaction of the knife—a gift from my daughter—balanced in my hand, the Zen of chopping vegetables, how my hand worked while my mind slid away, still focused on the task, but released, a kind of floating rest, attentive but soothed. That moment expanding to fill all time, the inner calm a place from which I had to be recalled.

———

Or not even about speaking, but about feeling my way in the dark.

———

My family were immigrants to the US from Greece and Asia Minor, one
side the remaining few who had escaped the genocide of the Ottoman Greek
subjects in 1922. The other side journeying to this country in steerage, with no
money, no prospects.

My grandmothers blessed our houses with holy water, they came to me in
dreams to announce my Fate to me. The tension between agency and destiny
infused every moment, every decision, every outcome: the lifted shoulder, the
gesture of my older relatives, saying "this is fate, we have no other option."

———

And now I am living through the unknown: house emptied, cabinets detached
and carried out, sink, concrete countertops removed, stove and refrigerator
gone, walls and ceiling demo-ed down. All my particulars—clothes, dishes,
art, books—taken out, handled by strangers who will clean them or deem
them ruined. This unknown layered on top of COVID-unknown, the layers
of not-knowing, the conflicting information about the nature of the virus, the
ineptitude of our national government, the politicization of keeping ourselves
safe, the inability of some to realize that their actions are actually not about
themselves but about protecting others.

How can I write an essay now without addressing all these things? Without
saying that we didn't need to be here?

———

And in the process of writing, that same trance, to enter an eternal present, a
focus that quiets the din around me, the static inside. Such a relief, time arrested
and the restless movement of my mind stilled, but alert to the uncertain terrain,
trying to find my way. As I go about the day, being pulled back over and over,

my mind sliding toward whatever I am working on, a movie running behind my eyes, part of me attentive to it even as I speak with someone else.

———

Easy to be fearless when not actually confronted with danger, when the threat is abstract. When the charred remains smeared across the ceiling, the wall taken down, the insulation hanging from the ceiling are in someone else's house. When not facing The Great Erasure.

———

I should be talking about the pandemic here. About literary ancestors. About the power of language. About writing against silence. But not caring about what I "should" do? An artifact of age. And the tiresome sense of "my" experience—who cares? That's another artifact.

———

Perhaps every writer feels the world's indifference at some point. Another "bridesmaid" response to risky work that editors profess to love but deem too "female"—whatever that is—to publish. Perhaps it is an absence of community, the act of writing so solitary, that makes the lack of response resound so loudly. But as an older woman, those moments of perceived indifference are akin to the moment—back when we went into stores—when I ask a salesperson a question and he turns to address the answer to my daughter, a young woman who didn't even hear the question in the first place.

———

The last thing left in the living room was the *mati*. Hung on the wall next to the large mahogany front door from 1926. Except the piano: upright, carved, an heirloom in someone else's family, a gift to me from my partner to ease the sting, years later, of my own family heirloom, a black Mason & Hamlin baby grand, that my parents sold. But the piano, muffled in plastic, stood mute, and what I saw was the *mati*. Round disk of deep blue glass—so soothing to the heart—the stylized eye of blown glass in the middle, swirl of white, dab of black in the middle, this one with the σκόρδο— garlic—hanging from it, that my mother had brought from Greece as protection for our home: years ago, a different house, before she died.

———

As an older woman, I am part of the process of being written out that our culture constructs. And maybe I've made a series of choices—given too much attention to toxic academic colleagues, resisted the idea of writing as a career, etc. etc.—isn't there always a list?—that helped create a sense of invisibility. Maybe it is impossible to choose when such expectations are heaped upon women as implied labor. But it is also an artifact of age. The impulse to hold the self solely accountable instead of naming the cultural ethos is a trap, a role given often to women.

So I negotiate that conflict: getting something down on the page while feeling erased at the same time. Questioning the purpose becomes part of the process: why do this? why continue to participate in a system that seeks to silence me? That insinuates itself into the process, threatening to derail it. Even writing this here, in this essay, is a risk. And if not to me, then to another woman. Or another. Or all of us.

———

Friends have expressed personal grief at the destruction of our kitchen. Heart of the house, we've gathered there for countless meals, cooking together or sharing meals or cleaning up afterward. For fifteen Greek Easter celebrations, we've cracked red eggs against each other's eggs for luck, the counter piled with roast lamb, spanakopita, *tsoureki*, the Easter bread scented with orange and *mastiha*. The celebration of resurrection, so central in Greek culture.

Because in Greece, things happen: large things, of course, the invasions, the wars. But everyday things, too: the truck parked in the lane lets go its brake and inexplicably, rolls backward to crush a boy. You wake from the traditional afternoon nap—as you have every day of your life awakened into the daily routine—to find smoke filling the air, soldiers on horseback galloping through the narrow lane. More exposed, more at risk, the veneer of safety, of everyday life an illusion, the veil so easily ripped away.

———

And on those occasions that I cooked with friends in my kitchen, the room buzzing with talk, that center point of stillness from which I worked in the room bright with exchange.

———

Even as I put words on the page: words as smoke dissipating, rising from the page and drifting away. Perhaps not erasure, but a deeper understanding of our fragility, of everything as provisional, the power of language not strong enough to allow purchase.

———

Kerostasia: the weighing of *keres*, literally. In *The Iliad*, Zeus (who, incidentally, is perennially young) weighs two "fateful portions of death" to determine the fate of Hector and Achilles. On the one hand: that no matter what we do to avoid it, our Fate will find us. Greeks believe in the dynamism between fixedness and flexibility, which is to say, between destiny and free will, a tension that causes the narrative of our lives to shift back and forth. Or, at least, we allow ourselves—in certain moments—to believe (or delude ourselves) that our actions have agency, that we can determine our direction.

———

So, not the threat of annihilation, really, but indifference, the fascination of the next bright shiny object that the literary culture has absorbed from the larger American culture—a turning away from what it fears—as a poet friend remarked to me. And that indifference affects all of us, not just those who fall into this specific demographic. It pervades our culture, and so, muffles every one of us.

———

Invisibility does have its merits, its creative freedom. The past several years I've been staging a hybrid work of poetry and theatre, and so, I have been immersed in the world of performance—its immediacy of feedback, direct interaction with performers and audience—collaborating with different communities, relentlessly external, visible. Exhilarating, yes. Terrifying, yes. And the need to retreat, to nurture an inner life, to sit alone and unseen, rises, so palpable, an almost physical yearning.

———

Writing now, as it has always been, as sustenance and resistance: ambition placed *in* the work, rather than *for* the work: still the deep trance, the exploration into the unknown, a way of staying present, of trying to see, to map a path into uncertainty, to explore the spaces between the things of this world.

———

The *mati* protects against the Evil Eye, the curse that brings destruction upon us. But the Evil Eye is not always cast by the enemy. Rather, it can be a friend or acquaintance, who envies what you have, who covets your good fortune, your beautiful house, lovely baby, publications, job. It is important to check that emotion, to examine envy, to be sure not to loose the Evil Eye on your loved one or friend.

If someone praises your accomplishment or remarks on the beauty of your child or compliments your home, the tradition is to make a symbolic gesture to ward off the Evil Eye. To stay safe. Perhaps I did not catch it, the moment someone set the Evil Eye on my house. I did not make the ritual gesture.

———

Writing still the "stay against confusion." But, no longer the illusion of permanence or leaving a mark in the world.

But writing as joining the impermanence, taking part in the fragility, understanding that, if I am not vigilant, my own hand might take up the eraser.

BESIDE THE MAN

BRET LOTT

All the traffic that I have in this with the public is, that I borrow their utensils of writing, which are more easy and most at hand; and in recompense shall, peradventure, keep a pound of butter in the market from melting in the sun: —

"Ne toga cordyllis, ne penula desit olivis;
Et laxas scombris saepe dabo tunicas;"
["Let not wrappers be wanting to tunny-fish, nor olives;
and I shall supply loose coverings to mackerel."]

—Martial, xiii. I, I.

And though nobody should read me, have I wasted time in entertaining myself so many idle hours in so pleasing and useful thoughts?

—Michel de Montaigne, "Of Giving the Lie"

HERE IS A STORY:

In the fall of 2006 into winter 2007, back when I was a mere 48 years old, still only a child, my wife and I lived in Jerusalem. I was a guest professor at a university, and while we were there plenty of friends came for visits, giving us more than enough reason to see pretty much all the holy sites in Israel. But in January and nearing the end of our stay, we decided we wanted to see Petra, the ancient city carved into sandstone canyons, over in Jordan. Our friends Jeff and Hart from here in Charleston were visiting us then, and we spent one cold and sun-drenched January day hiking the bright and towering red stone ghosts of the ruins.

But on our way back the next morning there came a snowstorm, and we found ourselves snowbound in a taxi at the crest of the King's Highway between Petra and Aqaba, elevation 5,000 feet, hours and hours from our home in Jerusalem. Forty-five minutes after the driver called in our predicament, members of the Jordanian army—yes, the Jordanian army—suddenly emerged from the white all around us, having driven their emergency response truck as close as they could to us, then hiking up the highway to the cab. Jeff and I helped the soldiers push the taxi out of its snow-mired fix, the driver pulling away and driving off—he couldn't park and wait for us to climb back in, because we'd get stuck in the snow again, of course.

That left Jeff, me and five soldiers to walk a mile or so through a blizzard back to their rescue truck. Along the way we pitched snowball fights, America versus Jordan (I actually yelled that out as I reared back to launch a snowball, and was nailed in the shoulder before I could even let go), all of us laughing, talking—they all spoke English—and trying our best not to think of the cold and this wind and all this snow. Then here was the rescue truck, emergency yellow, sharp and big with its pug-faced grill and running boards two feet above the snow-packed road. We all climbed into the warm quad-cab, the driver inside and ready for us. Eight of us jammed inside, Jeff and I in the back seat in the middle, a soldier on either side of us.

Then one of the men in the front seat pulled from the floorboard a battered Thermos, another soldier produced from somewhere a stack of four thick glass tumblers, and the one with the Thermos poured out steaming hot tea, Jeff and I given the first two glasses.

I don't even like tea, but I cannot remember tasting anything as perfect as that sweet and strong hot tea, its steam immediately clouding over my glasses.

That was when Jeff, glass in hand, turned to me and said, laughing, "This is going to be a great story."

"Yes it will," I said.

We weren't even warmed through yet, not even reunited with our loved ones and that cab—the story of our being saved in a snowstorm by the Jordanian army wasn't even over yet—and already we both were thinking, *We have to tell this story!*

That's how important story is.

I am writing this because I want to write it. I want to tell it. I want to share this.

But even though the fact of story is so very important, I wonder who, once I am dead, will read what I have written.

Have I wasted time in entertaining myself so many idle hours in so pleasing and useful thoughts? Have I wasted time in writing stories?

I am not writing here out of my growing old. I am not. Though of course even saying such feels as though I doth protest too much. But it's not that. Really.

It's not that I turn 62 this fall, three years older than my grandfather was when he died, and only nine years younger than when my father passed away, me somewhere in the middle ground of The Last Few Years, according to the calculus of my own genetic soup.

And this question of who will read all the words I've lined up was never one to have entered my mind when I was younger. I simply wanted to tell stories. I could do that, and I enjoyed it. I wanted to find out what happened to the people about whom I wrote, whether in fictive form or in nonfiction, those pointblank stories about me and what I wanted to understand about that middling subject.

My wife tells me I am thinking too much of the end of things now. Of retirement, of giving up writing, of simply teaching and teaching only. Of growing old. Of dying. She tells me she loves me, and I believe her, but tells me, too, I have other stories to tell, other things to write.

Here is another story. A longer one but one I need to tell:

Each summer I take fifteen students from the College of Charleston to our sister city, Spoleto, Italy, to live for a month, and to write, and to read, and to travel. Spoleto is in Umbria between Rome and Florence, and while there, we all live in a fifteenth century farmhouse turned into six modern apartments that look out on the Umbrian Valley toward Assisi, a beige smear on a hillside in the distance. Each year we also take a trip together into Florence, spend a day on a walking tour, then that evening at a private wine tasting course. All very civilized, all very Florentine: the students must dress up a bit for the evening and carry on well-mannered.

One year not long ago, the wine tasting was led by Count Niccolo Capponi, who was to present us with three different wines from his family winery, Villa Calcinaia, in Chianti. The event was held in the second-floor offices of the walking tour company in the old city center, the room actually a salon with high wide windows and a low dais at one end, where sat the Count.

He was and is what you call a character: a resident and native of Florence (as far as the family records could show, they arrived around 1200), he spoke perfect English in a broad British accent and was funny and dramatic, quite immodest and a little off-color: a blend of Terry Thomas and Thurston Howell the Third. A professor of Political Science to different American programs located in Florence, and with a PhD in military history from Padua University and a fellowship spent at Yale, the Count held court for an hour and a half talking about wine, about wine critics, about military history, and about writing—he had published a number of books, most recently a re-seeing of Machiavelli as not the diabolically scheming fellow most hold him to be, but a bumbling political naïf who made bad choices every time.

I wasn't sure how the students would react to him, and at first the room was a little cold, what with his dramatic pauses and whispered revelations. But gradually they warmed to him, until at the end of the evening students were lined up asking him to autograph the bottles they had purchased of his wine. Attending the evening, too, was his wife, Maria, a gracious and sweet and, one got the feeling, *long-suffering* woman, and their six-month-old baby boy, Vincenzo, the two of them quiet in the back of the room while the Count spoke, Vincenzo in his stroller.

But right at the end of his talk, the Count asked if we wanted to accompany him on a little walk, that he had something he wanted to show us only a couple hundred yards from the salon. Of course we agreed, though we had no idea where he meant to take us—later, when we all compared notes, most of us expected he would walk us to some place we'd already been shown by the tour guide earlier that day, and that we'd all have to act surprised at where he'd brought us.

We left the salon and followed him. Once outside he put on his tweed jacket and lit his burled wood pipe—really—and walked down one alley and another, then crossed the Ponte Vecchio itself, a lot farther than a couple hundred yards. Once across the Arno, we turned left and followed him up the street that paralleled the river, and onto another that broke obliquely away from the water.

Maybe a hundred yards up that street, along a granite block wall, we stopped. There beside us stood a huge wooden double door, twelve feet high and reinforced with iron studs. We watched as the Count reached into his pocket, pulled out a set of keys, and opened the door, inviting us all in.

That was when I looked back to the granite block wall, and saw the plaque mounted there: *Palazzo della Capponi*.

This was his house.

He ushered us into the foyer, where yet another twelve-foot door needed unlocking, and then into the inner courtyard of the house, four stories high and dark and old and Renaissance Italian, with busts on pedestals high on the walls, and frescoes—frescoes!—on the walls, too. It was all difficult to process, what exactly was going on: we were suddenly inside some other world, to put it mildly, though we'd been walking around Florence all day long. But this was suddenly the real thing, a house where there lived a Count and his wife and their baby boy Vincenzo, and now Maria and Vincenzo appeared from inside the foyer, the Count and his family allowing us into their domain, their *palazzo*.

We stood in awe, snapping pictures of the courtyard, thinking, *This is it! This is what he wanted to show us!* But that wasn't it, there was something else he wanted to share, he said, and then we followed him to a wide set of stone stairs up to the second floor, high as the third floor in a house anywhere else, and then to the third floor, and along a dark gallery with windows on the left that looked out on the courtyard, huge ancient furniture beside us, old portraits of long dead people on the walls, and a suit of armor that seemed as natural a piece of decoration here as a lamp on an end table back home.

The Count had the keys out again and stopped at the door at the end of the gallery, opened it, and brought us all into yet another world: his office.

I don't mean here to be writing in a manner too romantic, or purple, or, simply, overawed. But this was a moment when one's hairs are on end, one's antennae are up, one's faculties are fully employed: this was *happening*.

We were now in a room maybe twenty by twenty with books everywhere, paintings stacked and leaned against the walls, old silk wallpaper water-stained and hung with more paintings, and everywhere books. A huge desk in the center overflowed with papers, an old lectern stood off to the side, a stained-glass window four feet tall leaned against a wall, an ancient chandelier hanging above it all. And books and books and books.

"Here's what we're after," he said, and reached up to a shelf on one wall lined floor to ceiling with white volumes thick as old library dictionaries or ancient Bibles. He pulled from the shelf a narrow flat box, opened it, and handed it to one of the students, Katie, a young woman too stunned at what was going on to say no to holding it.

"Of course it's in Latin," he said, "but it's a letter from Henry the Eighth to an ancestor of mine. That's his broad seal."

Inside the box lay a document about eighteen inches wide, maybe six inches long, affixed to the bottom of it a rather beat up looking piece of wax the size of an oblong coaster. We could make out some shapes and words on the wax. The first words of the document itself read, "Henricus VIII."

We passed the box among us at the Count's urging, who said, "History was meant to be touched, it was meant to be fingered. It's a tactile thing."

We looked at it, awed (that perfect word again), while the Count continued to bring down from the wall more of those white volumes, opening them, pulling out vellum-wrapped piles of papers: the family archives back to the thirteenth century.

And, finally, here is the point of this all, the end of the too-long path down which this story has taken me: The vellum pages that wrapped the archives were themselves pages of illuminated manuscripts. A religious text that had, at some point in history, been scrivened out by a monk bent low to the page for too many hours to number, then, perhaps centuries later, deemed inconsequential enough to be used to wrap the Capponi family papers.

The Count stood handing off bundles to us, the illuminated letters on the wrapping pages right there, right there. But only as meaningful to some archivist one day long ago as the wrap on a chunk of butter, or paper around a mackerel.

The Count showed us more things: a blue velvet bag brought from inside a hidden cubby hole in the lectern that held a couple dozen Florins, the coin of the realm back in the thirteenth to sixteenth century, and that were passed around among us; that stained glass window, which he held up as best he could against the window looking out onto the inner courtyard, and for which, he told us, he still had the receipt from 1526; the initiation program from the Order of Saint James dating from the sixteenth century, inside it a passage from the Psalms written in Hebrew. "Who here can read Hebrew?" the Count asked and looked around at us. One of the students, Gabrielle, raised her hand, rather shyly, and when he handed it to her and said, "Read it aloud, if you please," she tried to beg off. But finally, after we cajoled and begged her, she read it out to us, her Hebrew classes in preparation for her Bat Mitzvah finally paying off. We cheered her effort once she'd finished.

"What's your most prized item in this room?" I asked, and immediately he reached to one of the volumes, pulled it down and unwrapped it, brought out a folder, inside of which were ancient pages written in careful calligraphy.

"When you're doing research about a particular person," he said, "it's always best to research the person beside the person. The subject can oftentimes make himself out to be something other than he is. The man beside him can come closest to revealing the truth."

He then read from the piece of paper in hand, translating into English the Italian. It was a memoir piece by an ancestor of his who had been the right hand man ("I dined at his shoulder," the Italian read) for none other than Giulio de' Medici, later Pope Clement VII, who would one day commission Michelangelo to paint *The Last Judgment*, the altarpiece needed to complete his Sistine Chapel. The particular passage he read to us was of a morning when Capponi came to Giulio's to find him eating breakfast and Giulio looking up to meet his eyes "in a meaningful way." Giulio, once Capponi had come to the table, then told him, "Job would not have the patience to last a day with Michelangelo."

That is, first-hand evidence that Michelangelo was a royal pain, from none other than a Medici. Right there on that piece of paper, penned by the man beside the man.

Then we were finished. The Count thanked us all for coming and led us out of the office and back into the gallery, where he suddenly decided to take the helmet off the suit of armor and place it on the head of one of our students, Chris. "Try this on, old boy," he said—he really said "old boy"—and Chris did. More pictures were taken all around before he took it off and we headed back down those stone stairs to the ground floor and the inner courtyard. And as if to give us one more thing, one more thing, he brought out his keys yet again but this time crossed the courtyard to the opposite side we had come in, unlocked yet another huge wooden door, and opened it to reveal the Arno right there across the street, the Uffizi straight across the river. Florence, right out his front door.

We thanked him and thanked him, as if words might be enough but knowing they weren't, and then moved across the street to take a look at where we'd been. The Count leaned in the doorway a few moments, waved at us all and wished us well, then closed the door.

When we pulled our cameras out to take pictures, we all had the same problem: the Palazzo della Capponi, a beautiful rose-hued stucco, was too big to get in the frame.

We'd come expecting a talk on wine from a Count. What we didn't expect was the touching of Florentine history. We didn't expect word from Henry the Eighth. We didn't expect Florins in our hands.

Or the family-wrap a sacred text had become.

But this is what we found.

We stood there across the street from Palazzo della Capponi for a few long minutes, all of us looking out on the river, back at the palazzo, to the Ponte Vecchio to our left, the sun set now beyond it, light fading. Some of us tried to talk about what had just happened, others recognized words weren't enough. Then we broke up, went our ways for the evening. Each of us in wonder, I am certain, at what we hadn't expected and what we'd found.

I am writing this because I want to write it. I want to tell it. I want to share this.

But I have already written fourteen books. I have already written, I fear, too much. Eight novels, three story collections, three books of essays. A number I do not know of stories in journals, same for essays. Words are with me always.

But I must be honest. I must try as hard as I am able to be the man beside the man. To be the man beside *me* so as to come closest to revealing the truth.

I must be honest—of course I must be honest—and attest to how I tire of words.

I tire of the limits I have found inside my own writing, the way sentences and images will come out with the same words replicating the same gestures and impressions. I tire of the way I still do not know how to do this thing I have practiced so very many years of my life. I tire of the way a blank page, no matter how many I have filled, is still at its birth a blank page.

I tire of the way what I have written becomes something other than what I had intended when first I embarked. As, for instance, this essay, which kernel appeared by my walking through the living room toward the kitchen one evening of no particular consequence, and glancing at the bookcases there to spy not a book of my own but the spans of books there, the dozens, the hundreds of them lining the wall, and the subsequent moment of a shiver through me, small and irrelevant, when I thought, who, if anyone, has even read everything I have already written?

It was an ordinary moment. An evening of no consequence.

There was nothing about the King's Highway and the importance of story in that moment. Nothing of the Count and Michelangelo and Henry the Eighth, and an illuminated text used like yesterday's paper. Nor even Montaigne. There was only a momentary pause, there in the living room, a glance at the books lining the wall, and my thinking in the selfish way a writer thinks, the mercenary way, the egotistical and heartless way a writer looks at all things around him as possible fodder for the next foray into words, *One day I want to write about wondering if anyone has read what I have written.*

Then came a rereading of Montaigne's "Of Giving the Lie," and its pondering the valor and folly of lies, the bald-faced and covert hallmarks dishonesty leaves upon the soul. The way a book one has written can end up rewriting the author in a better light than he can ever be seen. "In moulding this figure upon myself," Montaigne continues after the quote at the beginning of this essay, "I have been so often constrained to temper and compose myself in a right posture, that the copy is truly taken, and has in some sort formed itself; painting myself for others, I represent myself in a better colouring than my own natural complexion."

I'd intended to write about who might have read what I have written. Then perhaps about how books one has written take the place of the writer's life, that lie written to replace the life written about.

I'd intended to write about lies. But I am trying here to write about the truth.

I am trying to be the man beside the man.

I am whining. I know.

But I have tired of the way what I intend to write is never what I write, and what I write is never what I intend.

While the man beside me tries to write, I am in The Last Few Years, and wonder more than ever who, once I am dead, will read what I have written.

Another story—the last?—because my wife tells me I have other stories to tell, other things to write:

My 55th birthday, seven years ago. "Double nickels," I'd kept saying and texting and emailing all day long whenever the fact of what day it was came up in conversation. Double nickels, I'd said, because it was a silly thing to say, goofy, old-school, dumb. Stupid. Annoying.

I am like that. I will drive something into the ground to see how far I can go before someone—generally speaking, my wife—will tell me to cut it out. She tells me to cut it out a lot.

And now I am late home from a charity golf tournament, though I am a golfer of no merit. I have golfed for fifteen years now and have broken 100 only twice. I have made three birdies in my life. Still I enjoy it, being outdoors and with friends.

But I had promised to be home by four or five and to make dinner, jambalaya, a favorite. When it became apparent how slowly the tournament was being played out, I'd texted Melanie I would be late, and asked if she would go ahead and start dinner. Our two sons and their wives and our two grandchildren were coming over for the festivities, and I'd apologized, told her I would be home as soon as I could.

Near six-thirty I make it in the door from the garage to the kitchen, rushed and apologizing for being so late. Zeb, our older son, and his wife, Maggie, are there with the grandchildren, Mikaila, age three, and Oliver, who is three months old and asleep in the black baby carrier strapped to Maggie's front. Sarah, our younger son Jacob's wife, is there too, though Jacob hasn't yet gotten off work, will be here soon. Melanie stands at the oven, peering in at the cherry crisp I'd requested for dessert, and the long casserole dish of jambalaya lies on the counter, ready and waiting.

So though I am late, no one is troubled, no one concerned. I am just late.

"Happy birthday!" Melanie says, and comes to me, kisses me, and the others all wish me a happy birthday too, hugs all the way around, and I give a kiss to the top of sleeping Oliver's head, there in the baby carrier.

Lastly, there is Mikaila, who jumps up and down, clapping. "Happy birthday, Grampa! We have presents for you!" she shouts. "We have presents for you!"

I pick her up then, the girl tall as any four-year-old, though she has just turned three, and settle her on my hip, her blond ringlets so much like Shirley Temple it's a cliché even to point it out. But I am her grandfather, so this cliché is my right.

"It's my birthday!" I say to her. "Double nickels!" I say, and Mikaila says, "We have presents for you!"

That is when her father, beside us here in the kitchen and wearing a crisp plaid office shirt and gray slacks—he is an adult, he has a job, he is married, he owns a home, he is a father, he is my *son*!—pulls his hand from his pocket and, grinning at me, slaps that hand on the granite kitchen counter.

He lifts his hand to reveal two nickels, dull gray, one heads, the other tails.

"I've been waiting all day to do that," he says in near a whisper, still grinning.

I'd texted him two or three times today, like everyone else, the goofy, old-school, dumb, stupid, annoying term, driving it into the ground and driving it again. And now here was my son, his daughter in my arms, turning the joke back on me. Calling me on my dimbulb joke.

I laugh and shake my head. "That's a good one!" I say to my son, then say again, "That's a good one!" and in one more effort to pass down my penchant for the dimbulb joke, to drive it into the ground even further, so deep it's handed on to the next generation in all its innocence and joy and blond ringlets and presents for you, I set Mikaila down, then take the two nickels, and press them both to my forehead, where they stick.

I bend down to Mikaila, point at my forehead, and say, "See? Double nickels! Double nickels!"

She has no idea what is going on, what this dumb thing her grandfather is doing. She only stands there, still with this smile on her face, looking up at my forehead, then me, my forehead again.

Then she twists just a little, still smiling, and looks me in the eye.

She says, "Oh Grampa, so silly!"

And now, here: In the span of a space break upon a printed page, my granddaughter is now ten, a pre-teen, she insists, and insists again. Her brother, Oliver, is seven, and wears glasses with bold blue frames, cooler than any glasses I have ever owned. I've worn them since I too was seven: 55 years now.

Another granddaughter is here, too. Noelle, child of Jacob and Sarah. A little girl now nearly three and who talks a mile a minute, and whose smile fills me up.

The man is writing this because he wants to write it. He wants to tell it. He wants to share this.

And though the man is tired of words and the way they lead him down paths he hadn't intended, reveal to him things he hadn't planned to say— what he hadn't expected and what he finds—the man beside the man writes that, in this self-same moment of being tired of words, words and what they show the man are what sustain him. The wonder of finding out what the man hadn't planned to know is what makes him write more.

While the man still wonders if he has wasted his life entertaining himself so many idle hours, and while the man still wonders who, once he's dead, will read what he has written, the man beside the man records the truth: Oh Grampa, so silly.

The man beside the man writes that there is no posterity. There is only story. There is only a writer, and the writing of that story, and of another, of all of them, as many as he can tell, until he is dead and there will be no worry over words. Or readers.

There is no posterity. There is no one reading what he has written after he is dead. There is only living to tell the tale.

Here, the man writes. Now.

Read this.

TIME MACHINE

ALEIDA RODRÍGUEZ

WHEN I LANDED IN THE U.S. as a child of nine, I felt I had not
only traveled in space but also in time. Though it was 1962, behind me lay a
nineteenth-century world of oil lamps, muddy rutted roads, and horse-drawn
carts, while before me flickered a vision so sleek and modern there were no
shadows and bright-green lawns sprouted cones of mist.

Time traveler became my invisible identity. Secretly, I searched for mentors
in movies like *The Time Machine* (1960), envying Rod Taylor his ability to
go back and forth, to witness and control the passage of time. Propelled and
buoyed by a utopian vision of the future, he set off, watching the rising hemline
on a mannequin in a shop window, then the shop itself disintegrating to dust
in an instant, the surrounding buildings crumbling and disappearing, replaced
by insect-like cranes scampering on skyscrapers. His present had succumbed
to shattered shards. But by moving a crystal-topped lever sharpened to a point
like a pen, he could also reverse direction and return to his intact and cloistered
world of waistcoats.

I yearned for that, a trip back—not to Bountiful but to a prelapsarian
time—before the rupture in my family caused by the Cuban revolution. I
longed for the torn pieces to fly back together like the presents in Christmas
home movies the foster family in Illinois played backward, the shreds of
bright paper magically materializing mid-air and, as if magnetized, adhering

to the boxes, the mystery made whole again. The full-blossom look of delight reverting to a bud of anticipation.

When Rod Taylor, disillusioned by the violent and apocalyptic future he has seen, returns to his library in Victorian times, he selects three books to take back into the future. His best friend and his housekeeper are left to wonder what books he had removed from the empty places on the shelves.

"Which three books would you have taken?" asks a pre–*Mister Ed* Alan Young, with red hair and absurd brogue. One year later, Young would appear on black-and-white TV as a Los Angeles architect with a talking horse. Could he have foreseen that?

Around that time, two years after my own arrival via Operation Peter Pan, my parents arrived in Illinois and our bus-station reunion was captured in the local newspaper. They worked multiple menial jobs and tried to learn a new language and navigate a strange culture by watching television, while pining for a lost land in color. My father, who'd never driven a car, missed his horse. To ease his entry to the new world, I interpreted Mister Ed's wisecracks, making my father laugh and forget. That's how I became a translator, evolving into conduit and buffer, speaking on their behalf with landlords, bank tellers, employers, and strangers who shouted into my parents' faces as if they were deaf. Though I had much older siblings, they turned down the job of interpreter and guide, and went their own ways. In a what's-wrong-with-this-picture way, on the dead-end road to the city dump where we lived, I taught my parents to ride my bluegreen Schwinn bicycle, the one I'd bought with the $39 I'd earned doing chores in the foster home and selling handmade potholders door to door. On my bicycle I aimed to transport them to a carefree childhood they'd never had; they squealed as I ran along beside them, holding onto the seat, my mother wearing rollers under a bandana, my father feverishly biting the tip of his tongue.

Simultaneously, as a way to decipher my own biography, I read the biographies of inventors on the shelf in the children's section of the library, beginning alphabetically because I didn't know where to start: Alexander Graham Bell, Thomas Edison. From them I got the idea to experiment, a logical application of my voracious curiosity. I began by gathering bits of food from the kitchen, placing them in jars in a corner of the damp basement I called my laboratory, where some turned green while others inexplicably bloomed pink. I read comic books and ordered cheap items from the back pages, such as a small tinny printing press. I learned you had to pick up the rubber letters with tweezers and place them backward if you wanted them to read forward on the page. That's also how I learned the origins of the phrase "minding your *P*s and *Q*s," because in lowercase they were easily confused. Slowly and painstakingly, letter by letter, I constructed the present.

This led me to chronicle my own family, writing what I knew about how we'd landed where we were, pasting down our passport photos, anchoring us in the moment because I couldn't fathom the future. I described the scratchy grey couch donated by the Presbyterian congregation, upon which I was writing. I had learned English only two years earlier, so there are the telltale misspellings of a neophyte. Compelled by my own mystery, I started reading mysteries. In the fifth grade I wrote "The Case of the Strange Painting," in which a painting has electronic eyes that spy where a priceless emerald is hidden. I then discovered books about secret codes and started keeping a journal, rendering my abuse in an inscrutable alphabet, lest the culprits find the book. Thus books taught me what to convey and what to keep hidden, what doors to open and which to keep closed in order to stay safe.

I avidly watched *The Time Tunnel* TV show as a teenager desperate to escape, itching to cast off the premature reins of adult responsibility and my nightly terrors. By then I was wishing to be catapulted not into the past but into a distant future—fast!—as fast as my childhood had vanished and my perfumed world had evaporated, first growing tiny below my airplane window, then erased completely by clouds. Like Rod Taylor in his time machine, little did I imagine what lay ahead.

Though books became my guides into and through the new world and its peculiarly irregular language (witness: *through, ought—enough!*), the question for me was not what books I would carry into the future but what books I would create. My books would contain a map of where I had traveled and what had conveyed me, keeping me afloat—poems like small rafts. My mind was replete with impressions, so many it was a dizzying kaleidoscope—fragments of color turning and turning, forming a picture then breaking apart.

In Jorge Luis Borges's story "Funes the Memorious," a young peasant, Ireneo Funes, is thrown from a horse, suffers a head injury, and is paralyzed. From that moment on, he can't forget anything, even the minute and seemingly insignificant. His constantly absorbing and cataloging mind could recall not only every tree in his small Uruguayan village but every leaf on every tree—as well as every limb in all kinds of weather and every shape of cloud. Every gesture, every word, every object—everything he had seen and heard—was archived and played forever in the cinema-cavern of his head.

I too had been thrown from a horse as a child while visiting an uncle's farm. My cousins and I had ridden three to a saddle-less horse far out into a field on a cloudless day when a sudden storm blew in. I sat at the back, precariously straddling the widest part with my short legs. The horse, spooked by the furious rain and cracks of thunder, bucked me to the ground. I hurt only my left hip, which ever after made a loud *crick* when I raised my leg in ballet class in the new world. But the images and sensations of that fall have remained, like a bone that aches during inclement weather.

When I was abruptly uprooted from all I knew without my consent or foreknowledge, I unwittingly vowed my allegiance to the past by remembering every detail of the world forever locked away from me. In the foster home, my dreams nightly walked me to my grandmother's house, following the impressions her sandals made on the silty soil left by the new suburb of concrete-block houses. Under the single sky, everything became a time machine, especially the natural world; though people disappointed and betrayed, nature never did. I memorized the exact red wrinkles inside the chalice-like blooms of banana trees from which I drank water. Any scented flower swept me back, like the conveyor belt at the tomato cannery behind my father's pink butcher shop, a dim redolent place I had wandered into when no one was watching. The magic spell of fat raindrops falling jewel-like while the sun shone brightly became a kind of faith. Nothing was lost to me but the return—like Ireneo Funes, who was barred by his paralysis from reentering the world he had committed to memory in all its myriad variations.

Critics who've reviewed my work often mention loss and nostalgia and an obsession with recreating the past. But given my journey how can it be otherwise? There's a good reason my collection of essays is called "Desire Lines"—a spot-on term I found in a dictionary of landscape architecture, meaning the dirt paths people make when veering off the paths planned by the designer. I've pursued my own impulses and desires, straying from anything predetermined because once I'd had no choice.

The Chilean novelist José Donoso once said that writers living in exile tend to reconstruct in faithful detail the land they've been expulsed from, like a miniaturist building a diorama. That hadn't occurred to me but I recognized the impulse to manifest a time machine on the page that would ferry me back to a lost land of beloved images, scents, and flavors: the transporting taste of anise syrup poured over ice shaved from an enormous block by the street vendor on an oppressively hot day. The steamy outline of my body on the cool marbled-green floor tiles. The chameleon fixing me in time with its wrinkle-hooded eye while changing colors at will like nebulous moods.

Sometimes these days, lines of text come drifting back to me and I wonder about their author—then often discover it's me, though I hadn't known I'd memorized them, as if I'd gone back and plucked my own book off the shelf for the future. Recently, this one from the poem "Cool Acres" in *Garden of Exile* (1999): "what piece of the future/ has become dislodged and is floating backward/ to meet her ahead of schedule." The "what," of course, is death, which I thought would happen to me by age 20. I don't know what made me choose that particular age, but I was convinced. The end-date was my escape hatch, a promise and consolation I offered my teen self, as if to say: don't worry, this violence and abuse won't be forever. I couldn't imagine a door opening to a world free of horrors because the wall before me was smooth and solid with no hint of hinges or doorknob. So I assumed my freedom would be gained via death. When I reached 20, I was astonished I hadn't expired. Every day after that I was buoyant and lightheaded, as if I'd abandoned my heavy body and only my spirit floated forward—like a runner who trains with ankle-weights and removes them on the day of the race.

The idea of invisible doors may be why I was fascinated by the cartoon segment on *The Alvin Show* called "Clyde Crashcup," which I'd watched at the foster home, belly down on the oval hooked rug. The eponymous character was an artist who wore a smock and a beret and clutched a palette. He had an assistant named Leonardo, who never spoke but whispered secrets in Clyde's ear. At the time, I hadn't yet learned that Leonardo was the name of a dead artist and inventor. And Clyde, though dressed like an artist, was a kind of arrogant buffoon. It seemed Leonardo, though silent, was the true artist. When Clyde, with the help of Leonardo, drew something, such as a door, it became real and could be walked through. I was riveted by the idea of creating a doorway out of nothing, with a few strokes—and that has never left me. A few strokes of a pen created my own doorway in the air, and I've walked through.

Now 68, I have ambivalently arrived at the present-future, though I'm still more comfortable in a bygone era. I've ridden in on the rickety conveyor belt of the past. For thirty-five years I've been the steward of an old house full of Los Angeles history, surrounded by vintage art and furnishings, with a library of old books, many of them signed by their now-dead authors. Maybe that's why I relate to period movies. But physical things don't last forever, despite our best efforts; everything succumbs to the ravages of time—that's why it's called *ravages* and not *restoration*.

What Rod Taylor finds in the far future is a race of lazy surface dwellers, indifferent Eloi youth who never work, have no curiosity, and feel no empathy. Yearning to understand them, he asks to see their books, but the shelves of ignored volumes disintegrate in his hands, unreadable. He is outraged: "What have you done? Thousands of years of building and rebuilding, creating and recreating so you can let it crumble to dust. A million years of sensitive men dying for their dreams … *for what?* So you can swim and dance and play."

In my current future, I am surrounded by a similar race of superficial Naked Emperors who claim to have mastered things they have not begun to understand. They strut around in false finery compelled only by a need for attention, not a desire to know. Like the Eloi, they walk an easy path they've had no hand in cultivating. Recently, in a so-called thesis online, one of them said, "Old writers should move out of the way and make room for us." Is space limited? Is there a quota? Are talent and skill rationed? What about the lessons of history, the inspiration of mentors? No one springs fully formed from Zeus's head; everyone has been shown the way by someone. That's how culture is created.

So I'm not drawn to yesteryear because I want to be a clueless youth again—been there, done that, and residence is overrated. Nor because I aim to avoid or thwart death by living in the past, but rather because—when I go—I prefer to take the long scenic route back home.

"Time Machine" first appeared in *Los Angeles Review of Books*, June 18, 2020.

UNTIL THE END OF THE WORLD

MICHAEL VENTURA

The light at the end of the tunnel
turns out to be a tiger's eye.

—Wislawa Szymborska

COCKROACHES SCURRY. A tiger lies still in tall grass for hours awaiting prey. I write. The cockroach, the tiger and me—we do how we are made.

How, why, and for whom do I write? Well . . . my mother used to say, "*Why* is a crooked letter." I finally believe her. "What happened?" is a better question, but it's hardly an explanation. Age 11, sometime in the sixth grade, in a working-class Brooklyn slum, the boy I was began to carry a pocket notebook in which he noted this and that; also, that boy discovered books. Either that year or the next I almost died of hunger. I don't know if my hospitalization made it into my notebook. But somewhere around then Clelia, my brilliant half-mad mother, noticed my notebook, realized the notebook had become a constant in my life, and said, out of her fog, very seriously: "Remember, words are music." I took that as seriously as she meant it.

Age 13, 14, 15, I'm telling people, "I'm a writer."

Age 74: I'm a writer.

So . . . sometime around age 11 I decided I needed a notebook and a pen, in my pocket, at all times. And for all these years that notebook, in whatever form, has been the single constant of my life. More constant even than my name. (Some still live who remember me as "Speedy" or "Speed" circa ages 13 to 25.) If, on my deathbed, I can speak, I shall ask that a notebook and pen be placed within my reach—even if I can never again reach. It's how I'm made.

To accept the mystery of oneself. Period. Without question.

That's fuck-all tough—or so I've found it to be, facing and accepting the mystery of whatever self that, from my mirror or from my dreams, calls out to be lived and recognized and accepted.

But the writing self—that in me which compels this craft, all its work and pain and grace—I accepted the writing self without question when I was too young even to realize it was happening. By the time I did realize, writing was rooted too deeply in me to disentwine. And, in that sense, this writing-self is *utterly nonverbal.* It compels the words but is itself silent.

Took me a lifetime to grasp that. This, alone, is proof to me of the worth of growing old.

Let's clear something up right away: If there is to be such a thing as posterity—for, as you know, we may soon face the end of our species—it is an entity with which I have nothing to do. The literary world hasn't had much truck with me nor I with it. From 1974 to 2014, I wrote for—well, at first they were called "underground" papers, then "alternative," then finally only "weekly": *The Austin Sun, The Los Angeles Free Press* [very briefly], *L.A. Weekly,* and *The Austin Chronicle.* I didn't expect to become that kind of writer; I never graduated from anything, so I certainly had no credentials. I was fortunate that my first editor, Jeffrey Shero Nightbyrd, asked only one question: "Can you write?" "Yeah," I said, "I can write." So, after years as a working stiff—typesetter, transcriber, odd-jobber—for the rest of my life I've paid my rent and bought my beans with my notebook and a keyboard. The writing life.

From 1983 to 2014, with the exception of one year or so, every other week I wrote a column called "Letters At 3AM," roughly 1400 words about anything I felt like. Often politics, often memoir, but, really, anything. I figure more than 700, but fewer than 800, columns—plus all the film criticism, features, what-all. A total of published pieces between 1500 and 2000? Something like that. And three published novels that passed from this world as quietly as a good death.

All those words are not words for any future I can imagine.

Most of us writers, our words don't outlive us by much—and, very often, we live longer than they do. There's nothing like tragedy in either fate. A truck driver is a truck driver only till the end of the drive.

So if it's not for posterity, why do I still write every day? For the same reason that a cockroach scurries and a tiger—one of the very few left—waits hours in the high grass to attack: It's how I'm made.

Writing is not what I live for, it's how I live.

Before my stroke I worked daily in three-hour shifts. At least two shifts, but three shifts, or four, or even five, was not unusual. Ask anyone who knows me well; I'm not exaggerating. In fact, it was a six-shift round, working 18 hours on three different projects . . . that's how I stroked out six years ago. Oh, I can still wiggle my fingers and toes, and I slurred a little for a while but not anymore (usually), but . . . I can't work more than two or three hours in a day, and not every day. I don't watch a clock. I don't have to: when I hit a certain unmarked limit I get dizzy and my head feels heavy and sometimes I'm not sure where I am. Time to stop. For then I know I must, *must*, stay kind of still, rest easy, go gently, because "old" for me was finding there's something you can't push against—not because you shouldn't, but because you cannot. That stuff you used to have, the stuff that did the pushing—it's not there anymore.

As I write this day, I am 74—which is to say, three months and five days into my 75th year. My medical records note a stroke (age 68) and what my urologist called "a bad cancer" (age 70–71). As to that, Jazmin and I went for a second opinion; this doctor's voice was strictly matter of fact: "You have one to three years." I've beaten his verdict by six months and counting, cha-cha-cha, but, even so, my life expectancy measures in the single digits.

One year? Seven? Four?

Quickly, but not so quickly as to preclude a final sentence? Slowly, with the equally awful prospects of incapable-of-speech or talking-too-much? Or do I die faster-than-quickly, gone before I hit the ground?

If I sound flip it's because I'm desperate.

That's ok. I'm used to being desperate.

I am desperately alive. An old man, not scared most days, doing his last things.

This Christmas past, Jazmin gifted me *Japanese Death Poems—Written by Zen Monks and Haiku Poets on the Verge of Death*, compiled by Yoel Hoffman. You might say Jaz has a challenging sense of humor; you might say she knows that, as the gospel paean says, there's no hiding place down here; you might say she daily dares herself to be brave. Also, she knows her husband—knows that the first thing that fool, being myself, will think is: If they can do it, I can try.

Imagine: To have such authority with death that you know the day and even the hour, and you write the poem and do, in fact, soon after, die.

Kozan Ikkyo, age 77, in the year 1360:

> Empty-handed I entered the world
> Barefoot I leave it.
> My coming, my going—
> Two simple happenings
> That got entangled.

Hoffman adds: "He wrote this poem on the morning of his death, put down his brush, and died sitting upright."

Every death is the end of the world because the world will never again be assembled in just the way one dying person has seen it. But since 1945 and the possibility of nuclear war, and with the ever-swelling threat of Climate Change— now the individual's death overlaps and foreshadows our species' possible death, until the end of my life and the end of the world are, together, not "two simple happenings," but an ever-present sense of abyss that steadily permeates the world. Is mine the last generation to live into old age? That question has been urgent since Nagasaki and Hiroshima; Climate Change has made it more so.

I write this in our small rented studio on a height above the Bear River. This rental has no stove—just a toaster-oven and a hot-plate—but Jazmin and I are content because look at what we see through our enormous window: the river, a wide swath of sky, and, between river and sky, miles of hilly forest. The Sierra Foothills. We've seen an eagle dive for fish. Bear-scat by the garbage can. (Jazmin's niece jogged a forest-trail and, on a blind turn, ran into a bear—I mean, bumped into the bear, the beast and the girl equally startled; as Ashley tells it, "They say not to run from a bear, but oh boy, I ran!") Neighbors spotted a cougar. We see, daily, incredibly white cranes, wild geese, and so many birds and plants that, to me, Bronx-born, are nameless. The closest fire was six miles north—a wind-change and all this would be ash, and us with it. I've felt the trees grieve. I know that the birds know so many of their kind disappeared last summer. My trembling is merely one reflex of a far greater trembling.

And the river I see from my decades-old typing table is always the river you can't step in twice.

Once upon a baseball season, manager Dusty Baker helmed a losing team into September. His guys were about to play a Wild Card favorite. Asked his chances, Dusty Baker smiled sort of secretly and said, "A dying animal will bite with its last breath."

I'm happy he said that. I often think of it. There's a sense in which I write now with my last breath.

As I say, I can't work for more than two or three hours, usually in the late morning and early afternoon—not the night-writing I did most of my life. That's ok. For some of us, F. Scott Fitzgerald noted, "it is always three o'clock in the morning."

What I write depends on the day and what's coming. "The Big Book," as I call it, a thousand pages (yes, that many) of essay-type stuff to be written until I die . . . I can't work on that this season, it's too demanding, and, though I have thousands of notes, so far fewer than 100 pages are done. Also, there's the monograph on silent cinema—that one is fun, I can do that in any sort of season. Also, *Edendale*, aka *The Dragon*, the novel I've worked for twelve years; it was going to be two volumes; I'm refashioning it to one because, well, I believe a double-digit life expectancy is beyond my range; but it's gotta be the right day to do that sort of work. There are various notes on the Gospels. Notes for political pieces. And there's the long poem I've been writing for half a century—finally finished the first volume; two more to go. Oh, and one other novel completed, in manuscript.

I write as I age because how would I not write? A line of Cavafy's: "I attend to my work and I love it."

In fact, Cavafy, in Rae Dalven's translations, has accompanied me since I was a kid, as in:

> Give—I say—all your strength to your work,
> all your care, and again—remember your work
> in your time of trial, or when your hour is near.

This is the sort of thing I've tried to live up to all my life. To fail to do so now, just because I'm old, just because I'm frail'ish, would be to imprison myself. Or should I gripe and cower because human society these days seems drastically more insane than usual? Dorothy Day was fond of quoting Teresa of Avila: "All times are dangerous times."

As for the *mishegas* of publishing—it's fair to say that The World That Calls Itself "The World" makes me tired. Aren't roughly 2000-ish publications enough? Rather, I prefer very much to leave these unpublished packets of pages, a little bit like leaving ghosts of myself, ghosts with their own fates, humble I'm sure, and quite apart from me.

I wake in the night—sip a whiskey—in a rocking chair! just like Fats Waller sang!—and I wonder about this and that and the other. Wondered about writing this piece . . . wondered at my affinity with the cockroach and the tiger, and how we must not run from words, nor from the fates that words mark.

For me there is only one appropriate benediction and it is all I have to say to Life as I leave it: *Thank you.*

And . . . well . . . who, better than a writer, can more fully admire the breadth and height of those two so-often-typed three-letter syllables,

THE END

MAYBE I'VE BEEN OLD MY WHOLE LIFE

ELYCE WAKERMAN

I BELIEVE THAT WRITERS have a sense of an ending from the very beginning. For what is writing but a will towards keeping, so that which and those whom we cherish will not end? Joyce Carol Oates said that writing was all about assuaging homesickness, and if you find, as I did, that urge to retain, hold onto through creation, then the work of the writer, from the get-go, is to capture via the art of re-creation.

For many of us writers, it begins with diaries. From fifth grade on, my favorite Chanukah present was the leatherette booklet a little larger than the palm of my hand that my mother would give me. Though the colors would vary from year to year, these compact receptacles of my daily impressions always came complete with lined pages and, most importantly, a lock. And key. (This was at a period of my life when I would remember where I hid the key.) Into the pages of my diaries I recorded the friendly and not so friendly exchanges with classmates, descriptions of the boys I liked and how they had noticed or ignored me that day, things my mother said to me that hurt.

I have a stack of my girlhood diaries in a royal blue plastic bin that I bought at Staples and that contains all manner of memorabilia. My chipping diaries are wrapped in a rubber band inside the box. Opening to a random page from my twelfth year, I came upon this: "Dear Daddy, I was up at Audrey's house. Boys! Boys! Boys! And what Boys! Gorgeous. I am not exaggerating. But they don't

even look at us, so what good is it? NONE! Tonight I'm washing my hair."
(I clearly wasn't into transitional phrases back then.)

That wasn't a typo: I addressed my diaries to my father. He died when I was three, and from that point became the idealized person I could turn to, trust, rely on. He gave me no back talk, neither scolded nor showed disappointment in me; he only loved and listened. From my earliest childhood, I had a sense of an ending—indeed, the reality of an ending—and a crucial one, and this relationship that ended provided me with a will to save. To write.

My first book, written when I was in my 30s, was called *Father Loss: Daughters Discuss the Man That Got Away*. It was a study of the effects of father absence on girls, interwoven with my personal story of growing up without him. My second published book, *A Tale of Two Citizens*, a novel, written when I was in my 60s, was a fictional account of my father's illegal entry into the United States. I wrote other books during my adulthood, but the two that the publishing world found most viable centered on my lifelong quest to retain this man whose love for me, and its loss, shattered and shaped me. I have been known to observe with irony that there is nothing wrong with our parents helping out with our careers; my father, after all, was surely the inspiration behind mine. Writing has throughout my life been my way of forestalling endings, probing their influence, and overcoming them. In *Father Loss*, I tried to understand the impact of my father's death; in *A Tale of Two Citizens*, I gave him a life.

Two unpublished manuscripts that sit in the cabinet in my office examine the young lives of my grandmother and mother. Always, my creative impulse has taken me to the imagined stories of those I loved and lost. That's how I keep them.

As writers, the sense of an ending is what drives us. We chronicle, document, imagine so that we can forestall that ending. Beat it back. And, at least for me, age has had little to do with this impulse; it's been there all along.

Perhaps one distinction that comes with writing at an older age is the irksome experience of not being able to find the word I want to use. I can hear its syllabic rhythm, but I just can't get to it—and that is frustrating, and the only anomaly I can think of that affects older writers as we write. Maybe I'm forgetting the others.

Now, with the Coronavirus upon us, the prospect of my own death does loom larger. And so do the hours and days in which I have time to write. An ironic coincidence in terms of this discussion: there's more time because of the prospect of there being less time. But unlike the apprehension I have felt in recent years whenever making a nonroutine purchase that it may very well be my last car, notebook, sheet set, I don't, as I write these words, feel that they may be my last.

THE RED CRAYON

MONA HOUGHTON

I FOOLED AROUND with writing all through high school and had an especially wonderful teacher in twelfth grade. She gave us exercises asking us to describe eating ice cream and set that against a fight with a sibling, that sort of thing. It was the late sixties. At night, after my parents had turned in, I would sneak out, smoke some pot and then hop back through the window and set out to complete these exercises with a kind of stoned reverence. I loved the whole marriage between being high and making things up.

In college I took a couple of creative writing classes, and a story I wrote actually got published in the school's literary magazine. That was a kick, a real boost. Then I stopped going to college and had to work, but I still wrote; I'd write before the workday began and at some jobs I'd write while pretending to do my work. I'd write and write.

I also read like a maniac. I'd go to the old library on Ivar in Hollywood and come home weekly with a stack of novels. And I'd read them, indiscriminately. Mostly contemporary, mostly American. All the while I had this vague sense that it would be grand to make something that someone would respond to the way I responded as I plowed through all these pages. But it all felt like a pipe dream. And then I read *Kin Flicks* by Lisa Alther. (I haven't looked at the book in forty years.) I don't know why, but I think it was that book, that specific book, that made me firmly commit to being a teller of tales, to set out and actually spend a significant portion of my life, at least a part of each day, making things up, making fictions, telling stories.

And I did it. I went back to college, took more classes, ran into another wonderful teacher, started publishing short stories here and there. Flash forward and I've spent decades writing. I've had jobs too, writing jobs, teaching jobs, job jobs. No matter, if it wasn't in the foreground it was in the background; I was always writing.

I am not what anyone would call a successful writer. My publications are minor. And there have been years when this bothered me. I had had high hopes, sure. Then sometime in my mid-60s I realized my relationship to the writing had shifted.

I approach it now, not with the expectations of publishing or seeing a novel I wrote in a bookstore window, but with the expectation of pleasure, the moment to moment pleasure I get out of making a sentence that begets another sentence . . . in the story that emerges, a story that may only have an audience of one. That isn't to say I am not writing to be read. I still want to publish, I still want to share what I make with other people, I still have the want to make in someone else the kind of escape, that leap into other places where fiction has always taken me, but if this part of the equation never is, I still have the making part and that transports me.

Thinking about this sends me back to my first real encounters with books. My parents read to me and my brother a lot, nightly is my memory. *The Wind in the Willows*, *Mrs. Piggle-Wiggle*, I could go on and on. *Harold and the Purple Crayon* is certainly the first book I remember reading on my own. But my favorites were always *When We Were Very Young* and *Winnie the Pooh*.

When We Were Very Young had a pink cloth hard cover, and the first letters of each word on the front board were big and in a fancy font. I adored the object, the book itself, its smell and feel, and I absolutely loved the way the words, as they were read to me, made me feel, where those words took me. So much so was this love, so huge, I remember taking the book and a red pencil (or was it a red crayon?) and a pair of snub-nosed scissors and secreting myself in the closet and taking terrible liberties. I remember the tortuous pleasure of marking the pages and cutting them willy-nilly—knowing full well that each action would have wild recrimination, for books were not to be manhandled, were to be treated as sacred objects.

I am sure some punishment befell me for this, but I don't remember that at all; I do remember coming out of the closet, I do remember fearing discovery, but what stays with me, what is concrete and lasting, is that sheer and unabashed pleasure I experienced as I interacted (for lack of a better word) with the *object*, the book. I somehow had penetrated its surface, I found out, through cutting and marking, how it worked. So whatever spanking or "go to your room for an hour" came after discovery is lost in the folds, but not the action of the affair, which is still as vibrant in me as the moment I woke up this morning.

And so, writing to me now has much more of the bliss of the closet in it than the bliss of the afterglow. I want to pull myself apart, take a red crayon and blue crayon and push the waxy colors across the page and see what in the end emerges. I want to make the words on the page sing what is rambling through my mind, I want to make some sense, I want the pieces to cohere, to cut and cohere.

This is where writing lives in me now as the end of my seventh decade approaches.

IN MY 7ᵀᴴ INNING LET ME RISE LIKE LAZARUS

E. ETHELBERT MILLER

I WAS DISMISSED from Howard University five years ago, after forty years of service. Budget cuts and age discrimination probably went into the decision making. Or maybe it was because I never signed up for one of those early retirement packages that colleges tend to offer. When college administrators talk about transparency, I think immediately of the "Middle Passage" and what slaves were never told. So, there I was one May day, moving my boxes from the African American Resource Center. A few hours later I was sitting in the ballpark watching the Washington Nationals. I was staring at the peaceful green outfield, feeling as meditative as Thomas Merton. In the last season of my life I find myself turning to baseball for solace and perhaps insight into what the "score" really is these days.

When I turned 50, I wrote my second memoir, *The 5ᵗʰ Inning*. In baseball, a game played for five innings can go into the record books as an official complete game. A game can end because of inclement weather or lights failing. Too many of my friends died in their 30s and 40s, never reaching 50. Cancer, AIDS, suicide took them. Others "died" when they were laid off. Escorted from their office and workplace as if they had joined a funeral procession. There are many ways to die.

It's now 2020. I will turn 70 in November. My 7ᵗʰ Inning. When a friend turned 70, I wrote this poem for her:

The 7th Inning Stretch

Let me rise like Lazarus.
Let me bask in the sun with my fellow fans.
Let me sway with the music.
Let me point at the scoreboard and ignore the score.
Let me wave my cap.
Let me open my arms and embrace my last inning.
Let me celebrate baseball.
Let me celebrate life.

This year I was planning on having a big birthday celebration. A gathering of friends . . .

This was before the coronavirus pandemic, before the global paradigm shift. So much suddenly changed. Too many people have died. Relatives as well as friends.

Maybe we fell through a trapdoor on January 26, 2020, when Kobe Bryant died. His tragic death, along with his daughter and friends, shocked us. Now as I write this, there is no basketball, there are no sports.

We wear masks. We no longer touch. We only continue to die.

Yet, as the South African poet Dennis Brutus once wrote, "somehow we survive." Like blues singers we discover the resilience of Blackness at the core of life. We learn to live and love despite heartbreak and loss. As a writer, my responsibility is to uphold the singular voice within the communal chorus.

When you reach 70, it's important to turn knowledge into wisdom, to become a pillar within one's community. These last few months I find writing and reading opens the door to spiritual contemplation. One book I turned to was Richard Wright's *Haiku: This Other World*. During his last years Wright cultivated a garden and wrote hundreds of haiku.

I enjoy embracing the haiku form and structure during this time of social distancing. I use solitude to connect with myself and to enhance my appreciation of nature. My time is spent working in my backyard, raking, trimming trees, pulling weeds, and sweeping. Last year I added a statue of the Buddha to instill a degree of tranquility to my space. I'm often inspired when a bird sits on his head.

> how lonely my arms
> trees walk away from the wind
> i now hold nothing
>
> your hair turns silver
> like waves cresting at the beach
> love endless like sand
>
> hug the open sky
> flowers bloom when they are loved
> the birds are flying

Sitting meditation is why I like baseball. The slowness of the game. Time stops when a batter steps out of the box, or when a pitcher waits for the signal from the catcher. For the fans sitting in the stands, time is measured by outs, runs, and innings. The ballpark is where one can find the soul of our nation. It is why we honor Jackie Robinson as much as Martin Luther King, Jr. It is why I return to baseball in this last season of my life.

Baseball is the game that begins and ends at home. It's where rookies and old timers meet. It's where records are broken and retirement is inevitable. Baseball is the celebration of the moment. It's the game you don't want to look away from. What you might miss is the timely hit or the amazing catch.

When I sit in my backyard reading or writing, words amaze me. So has aging.

Each morning I "read" my face in the mirror. My hair becoming grayer, wrinkles sprouting from stress, my body slowly slipping away to avoid staring at my nakedness.

I am the only member of my immediate family still living. There are four graves at the Mount Hope Cemetery, Hastings-on-Hudson in New York. My brother is buried with our father, my sister with our mother. There is no grave or space for me. I suspect it was planned this way. I was once the forgotten baby, the child almost given away. Maybe I became a writer because I never really knew who the people I lived with were. They all kept secrets, they all suffered from loneliness and degrees of depression. They were all trapped in the stories of the Old Testament, afraid and somewhat superstitious, and being punished by a God who protected them but never answered their prayers.

In the early sixties, my brother went off to a monastery looking for God. He returned home monk shaven bald. There was sadness in his eyes. It was my brother who read my first poems. When he died in his early 40s, I knew it was from a broken heart. Where was the "new" Testament for him? Why did my brother suffer for being so black and blue?

My sister died the day before her birthday. She would have been 73. She is the only person I had to be a caretaker for. Moving her from New York to DC was not the journey south she wanted to make but illness carries its own map. I watched as my sister's health declined, her beauty fading with her memories. I'm glad she could still remember my name before she departed. My sister is the only person I have ever watched die in front of me. In the hospital, my hands feeling her body turning cold. A nurse closing her eyes.

> leap into beyond
> the seasons change with each breath
> there is nothing here

I will soon reach the age my sister was when she died. I feel like Joe DiMaggio trying to extend his hitting streak. Will I die within the next two years? Will I break my sister's record? Will I reach that 8th and 9th inning?

It's baseball that has taught me how to deal with swinging and missing. I no longer have a desire to win a major literary prize or even submit work for publication in journals. I write for tomorrow's readers. I write for the people who live alone. I write for the person whose lover has left. I write as elder and witness.

Earlier this year I joined a small delegation organized by the Washington Office on Latin America (WOLA) that went to our southern border to assess the condition of migrants coming to America seeking asylum. It didn't take long for me to understand that the people I was meeting probably had the same hopes as members of my own family who came to the US from Panama and Barbados in the 1920s.

Every migrant has a story. Too many, however, become trapped in history's dreams.

As I move towards becoming 70, I'm also moving towards "home." Not a place but more a destination beyond the horizon or somewhere maybe not even outside but perhaps deep within my heart. For now, let me call it desire.

When I sit and write my haiku, the lines being slowly sipped, the syllables counted, the moment is similar to keeping a scorecard. What just happened? Did I get it right?

Is a wrong word a recorded error? I want to practice the simple joy of celebration before I can no longer describe what I see.

I believe poets should live long lives. I celebrate poets like Stanley Kunitz and Donald Hall. I remember being on the Bennington College campus in the 1990s and seeing Hall walking with Robert Bly. They were two old bards sharing a couplet of friendship before going off into the dark night.

Too many of us will die alone. I hope my writing will visit me during my last days.

May I be blessed to read one of my early poems and remember my youth. It is saddening to see so many elderly people suffering quietly in nursing homes. No one should die in the absence of beauty.

My poems will one day become my fingerprints. They will be the evidence that I was here and struggled with all matters of the heart. My poems will be the evidence that I attempted to touch and desired to be touched. My poems will say "I love you" to readers and listeners and they will outlast all my lovers and would be lovers. And then I will rise when my words are spoken.

Haiku 8, 19, 20, and 28 used in this essay are from Miller's forthcoming haiku collection *the little book of e.*

OLD AND UGLY, UGLY AND OLD

HOLADAY MASON

How could anything bad ever happen to you?
You make a fool of death with your beauty.

—Florence & The Machine, "Hunger"

1.

What I recall about the man my mother went to visit who lived up Latigo
Canyon was his skin. It matched perfectly the grayish brown hue of the hard
California dirt where his organic farm, like a lopsided garden of Eden, cut a
zigzag pattern of pathways up the steep hillside of the canyon and flourished.
And a lot of his skin was showing, since he wore little clothing, maybe a
loincloth or a speedo. He had reams of elephant skin. It hung from a frame that
showed bone and muscle in uncannily equal measure. I remember his skin, and
the remarkable fact that he drank his own urine daily, with the conviction it
would maintain his young visage, his health, his virility. He saved his urine up
throughout any given day, and then drank it like nectar, a special tea concocted
by personal DNA, a private and self-contained golden fountain of youth.

To my 8-year-old self, he was a slim fairy tale creature, moving with
studied assurance between rows of organic citrus trees heavy with huge grapefruits
large as the heads of newborns, green beans like the crooked fingers of giants,
avocado fruits like bats hanging in the dusty deep green leaves of his orchard, all
sorts of herbs and strange driftwood objects clanking in dull yet reassuring tones
from the trees, pieces found I assume on the shore of the Pacific Ocean just a mile
or so west of what was then a hippie habitat for increasing longevity.

I was red-faced, prone to overheating, a freckled child uncomfortable in my new little body, and he was curiously terrible and wonderful at the same time. He was very, very, very tall, and supposedly intended to help my mother as she grew afraid of her own aging, those last years of her menses—what I call the blood days, which make women a pheromonal paradise for men, since, during those years of bleeding, we smell of sex, permanent robust endless possibility, procreation. We smell of eternal youth. She had to be pretty scared of something to have dragged a sunburned 8-year-old up into that hot, dusty California canyon. She wanted what he had. He had his *thing* figured out and was not conforming to anyone or anything. This was clearly elegant, powerful. Pow-er-ful.

2.

The word *ugly* is from Middle English / Old Norse *ugglier*, meaning "to be dreaded," from *ugga*, "to dread."

3.

When I was a young woman, I was beautiful, but never knew I was. What makes youth so attractive is its smoothness. It is so silky, like balance, that qualitative sense that one can never break into globby, boney bits. Yet, I broke when I was very young. Living deep in the country with other teens sent away from home for lack of fitting in (there was even a poor kid who had tried to rob a bank), I did not know the perimeter of my own form. I felt limitless and powerful. My body seemed flexible and possible, like a cloud or a shape-shifting snake. I was a pagan gypsy in cutoff Levis, midriff-baring halter-tops barely covering brand new breasts.

In the early part of spring, when the winter gray was still on every scrub oak branch and each moss-coated granite boulder, we teen wildlings would gather manzanita, which burned hot, and oak, which burned long, skimming the forest for fallen branches. We built enormous heaps of dried logs which we lit in that age-old earth-based way, fanning and feeding flames into mountains of fire that, like youth itself, lapped the unlimited score of the night as if to tease and flirt with our message of indomitable, supple strength. The bonfire, gracefully high, lit the black scope of the sky with heat and durable sexual propulsion. Fire—gorgeously wild.

One night, in a heat, I ran down a steep hill while the boys not yet men drummed and played guitar. I gathered speed as gravity took over my thighs, calves, feet, and I leapt with youth's hubris over what in my memories seems still to be a towering bonfire—a blaze of driving flames. I ran down that greening hillside soaked with spring rain and tiny new wildflowers curling up to the still-freezing weather, I trampling their heads, breaking off buds, barreling fast and hard so speed would allow me to fly over the top of the fire.

But the body is a solid mass, unresponsive to themes of omnipotence. My landing was hard and wrong. I was at that age where what other people of the same age think is oh so important, and I was ashamed of my limits, so I limped away, hiding pain as well as injury. That night in April, I blew out my anterior cruciate ligament, and, unbeknownst to me then, I saddled my older age with multiple surgeries, all born of that one youthful miscalculation. It happens. I really wished I could fly. Still do. We do. But breaking makes us what we are—or, rather, the mended parts, the bits one must tend over and again to keep growing, moving, accepting, living.

At 60, I am now breaking a little at a time, with "severe bone marrow edema—moderate compression fractures, loss of height of the L1-L2 intervertebral disc," etc., etc., the winnowing of drying branches at the ends of the limbs. We do break, proceeding either to luminous surrender curiously attending or aggravated private protests and self-pity, often alternately all through a given day. My elder cat just sleeps more and more, snoring in triangle-shaped expulsions. Eventually, I suppose, we will all do something of the sort.

4.

Writing in youth for me was about holding that fire inside before it burned more things down: the agile pirouettes of being able to address my current emotional velocities and madness, the act of making beautiful images and language from mental-emotional states, even to the point of dazzling or seducing myself or others with beauty, with language clever or earnest.

That goes a long way, that drive, that wish to be seen, to be relevant—to exist, really. The wish to have some way to bring heaven down to the page or manage with hell, any or all of the concerns of a human life. Containment was one of the engines of my early writing. The other was more ephemeral. I heard poems like voices in my body and had to write the words down, whether they fit an acceptable poetic form or not. In fact, I eschewed form in order to listen more closely for that "voice," following and falling in love with the seam between the non-physical, ephemeral-universal and the personal-emotional, ever curious to see where I was led by something that felt of but was not of my self.

I wrote first in order to survive, then because I wanted to exist. I wrote because I had to. But one had to achieve, even seduce in some way, in order to belong, to be heard, to be someone, to be accepted by the literati. Such are the ambitions of the world and success.

5.

Youthful beauty, its driven certainty, does not fill us with dread. It allows us to dream of an eternal buffet of possibility that guards us from the experience of uncertainty, choice, limit. Youth is the plumpness of expectation. Our allotted time has not yet dwindled; that isn't even ever gonna happen. No, youth is the surge of beckoning. Come hither into me, crash into me, rock and roll for sure. Sex. The vagina, after all, is a doorway into the eternal rose of fecund procreative *wowza*, no thorns on the stems. We believe we can multiply, seize, and sustain our own existence. The prowess of being able to make things happen in the world, to matter in the world of course, is the opposite of letting the ambitions of the world go. So we love power, really. Beauty is powerful. Youth is not ugly, not dreadful, not yet anyway. On that bonfire spring night that formed me with my not even knowing it, I got up from that injury and went on running daily for years, unaware of what things can cost.

Aging is the antithesis of patriarchy. Aging recalls us to our powerlessness, our temporary state. We dissolve and cannot sustain power inside the tyrannical demands of form, personal or popular agendas. Ageism is preceded by sexism. Dependency means limits and vulnerability. And the vulnerable can only be safe in a realm where kindness, rather than status, is valued.

Old bodies are less symmetrical. We dip and sag and hang and buckle. But why do we find it dreadful and therefore repulsive? I ask this question while I continue to avoid beginning a series of nude self-portraits I planned to start three years ago, one image to be shot every month until I can't do it. Then, like Lucian Freud, who painted his mother aging before, during, and after her death, as an homage to the home her body had once been to him—like him, my notion is that when I no longer can shoot the self-portraits, I'll have arranged for a brave soul to keep shooting me, even after I am a corpse. Self-portraits, I think, might help me, or maybe force me to look at what IS, not what I want, what I wish for.

My avoidance is dread. But is it dread of ugliness? Or, like writers' block, is it fear of being obsolete, of being invisible when the force of youthful voices with the next popular topics, politics, and style is so much louder? Is it fear of being relegated to the slush pile of irrelevance, of being unable to compete? And to whom I am supposed to be relevant? Why would the muscles of staying alive, not just alive but enlivened, why would that not be a viable conversation to engage in?

6.

I know a man who, in his late 80s, is still winning awards for his design work. His age has consolidated his sense of beauty. Many writers and artists grow wilder and stronger with the years, circling and digging deeper into the soil of their own idiosyncrasy. They become the form that the young writers and artists study—as one friend said (and he took this from someone else, of course), "steal from the best." Really, we all have teachers and lineage, but there is something in this modern time of Internet that loathes the body, eschewing real feeling and form, as if we can become intangible beings subject to no more than the whims of popularity. So it is not about writing, painting or the making of music that daunts us, but the flood of pseudo-innovation. We live in a crazy world. Now all generations say this—all of us old folks talkin' 'bout those young folks. Yet with the advent of the Internet, it is harder to tell the real thing from the Memorex (remember that?)—so too with art, and certainly with writing.

It's fashionable right now in first world countries for very young women to spend a small but real fortune to dye their hair platinum. All colors of women make their locks slate gray, silver, iron, white. I spent years dying my hair red or brown just to avoid the stigma of being an older, therefore socially less valuable, woman. It got so nuts I was running to my hairdressers twice a month where she'd put the dye in my roots and I'd just go home to work until I needed to wash it out. Maybe these young women want to try it on—being old before they are, sort of like wearing your mother's high heels when you're 6. Maybe they feel it's glamorous, like smoking used to be, or big cars. Maybe they fear that, with the world increasingly digitized and unreal, they won't exist long enough to not have to pretend. Perhaps there's a feeling that all human experiences are pretend, since truth and fiction are not clearly demarcated by time, space, the bodily nature of life—so maybe people are not real. Maybe we *are* versions of selfies, Photoshopped into a make-believe eternal youth of excitations and seduction. If this is true, how do we find writing and art that is communicating a depth of human experience and not just an outcry of faux emotion designed to get "likes," not popular or popularly politic, something more than a dazzle of forms and words with momentum, but words that have true feeling? And how do we know what true feeling is if we scrape our knees up kneeling primarily at the altar of what is popularly beautiful *and* digital?

7.

My knees hurt. My hips hurt. On Montana Avenue in West LA, whole stores are devoted to selling fancy magic water. It's about the glow: gold dust, stardust, the proverbial fountain again—sort of like the hippie farmer's pee bonanza, but certainly less fecund. Yet still I shy from my tripod, my camera, my pen. It IS frightening to see the truth, to face feelings, to feel one can stay relevant or have something to say. It is frightening to face limits, to look in the mirror, to run towards extinction, not from it. But now it seems more frightening to run away and risk missing the show.

I was at a famous writers' conference this last summer. It was the third time I've attended, yet with all its authentic generosity and rigor in terms of craft, many of the elders were bewildered. We felt useless. We could not spin the façade in agile competition. We were not popular or fast enough. We could not jostle our writing inside the kaleidoscope pinwheel of dazzling forms and causes. Our voices, I noticed, were frequently more subtle, more hushed— softer, less strident and jaw-dropping.

Older people often sleep less. Or wake in the night. We have the chance due to the limits of the body to move towards the nocturnal, into reverie attending the internal, the minute, and the small "ten thousand things" that make up each moment. We can move towards the large, the vista of perspective with scope. The things that we feel and care about in age approach subtly, and I hope we can see and hear them, to give them respectful due.

8.

We have lost many poets these last years. Recently, LA poet Holly Prado joined those beloveds who have left this world. Holly wrote poetry daily as a practice, as prayer, a meditation, a commitment to stay alive while still alive—to keep her soul like a loud and at times bold songbird, freshly in reverie while the cage of the body disintegrated. She made real poems about things that were near to hand: pomegranates, her husband's back as he wrote at his own desk, friendships that inexplicably ended, stone Buddhas, chocolate. The things of any life are important in as far as they are deeply experienced and honored. In the end, she was a no-nonsense gnome of a woman who kept walking with her walker and her dignity, completely human, small and piercing.

I had a dream right after she died. In it, she stood face forward in an enormous field of blooming goldenrod that covered her up to her collarbones, chin jutting a little forward in something that could be interpreted as a dare or a demand. Her lips never moved. In fact, she never budged, but her eyes were speaking, saying *Just keep writing*. Like the last of the Mohicans, "No matter what occurs, stay alive."

How many days do I say to myself, "Why write? Is there something new to be said?"

There is a lot people are saying that needs saying in many ways on all fronts of humanity. Staying really alive no matter what occurs. That is relevant and deserves voice. So do the voices of the elders. Since we will all pass this way.

9.

That giraffe of a man who drank his pee was neither smooth nor young, yet I remember him as if he were a god, marvelously large with the presence of ambition and certainty. He had that thing—his own opinions, his supremacy. He was not broken. Being broken fills us with fear and dread of the fact that we can be hurt, will weaken, wrinkle, will do all that and more. We will die.

Truthfully, I dread powerlessness. I do not like pain much either, although I know it well. Dependency is dreadful because of the very things that make youth so driven—the great dark yawning mystery of the void space of the unknown which is the feminine—that awesome, awful nothingness that precedes all things, the void we come from, carrying the energies and stamina of our youth. Aging is dreaded because it *is* the yin to the yang, the hold of the dark mother's womb, of the vagina—that terrifying place we all have to exit to get into this inequitable, gorgeous world, to get things done. It is that same void space we all must enter when we are done here. In the meanwhile, all human experiences have merit and can be offered as comfort, as teachings, as sharing, as reciprocity. Young or old, it's up to us to write it down, work it out, wake up midnight or daylight still curious, since we are all going to get there.

We are all going to the same place in the end.

JOURNEY TOWARDS A TOMB

MICHAEL C FORD

MY FIRST DIVE into the pool of prose fiction is a short narrative titled "Windshield Wipers Are Timekeepers in the Human Race." It reads as though it were extracted like a painful molar from a row of teeth in a mouth that, sometimes, speaks aloud about our personal travelogues towards the other side: going through the rainy dark Jack Kerouac attempted to stare into, searching for a way to see directly into the eyes of God. And, maybe, like many peregrinations through seasonal aspects, where anyone's mystic observations or sense of existential truth is very difficult to find in metaphoric rain in places where days are so dark they resemble nights.

However, when people ask: "Do you believe in God," I will respond with something like: "Not that God of white Protestant fundamentalism," meaning I could never adhere to the bearded avuncular un-nameable entity in the clouds trying to look my name up in a book so he can decide whether or not I deserve to take a spiral escalator to the main room, where William Powell is, playing the role of Flo Ziegfeld pondering choreography of a pink-frocked Follies segment for MGM or, as a grave alternative, motivated to just showing me the austere coal-chute, then shuttle me down into Dante's Inferno.

I imagine the god we speak of when we say God to be in terms of what the prairie Native Americans believed without any impediment of lame superstition: that is, a soliciting of the Great Father, the Great Spirit, the Creator of Being. The universal connection to a language-based spiritual adhesive is what Kerouac titled Scriptures from the Golden Eternity and, as a surrealist extension, however vague, we studied the 16th century search by conquistadors for the Seven Cities of Gold in Cibola.

Let me hasten to admit that any similar obsession of my own has been more related to an informal minimalist search for seven random LA suburbs, basically, within what had been indemnified as the Golden State of California. (This, of course, could be nothing more, perhaps, than enthusiastic protection of our tender ears from the more caustic albeit accurate criticism of our unfair state.)

One of Kerouac's bibles that, without question, inspired the conceits he assimilated to create many of his paragraphs for *On the Road* (1957) was Jack London's book chronicling his jumps from one hobo junction to another, riding the rails, sleeping in boxcars. It was a document of travel and survival in the 1890s titled *The Road* (1907) more than once, repeating the phrase *beating my way*: all the while resonating with Kerouac: an author, one is reminded, who became a middle twentieth century celebrity by insinuating the words "beat" and "road" into his literary concept of improvisational, lyrical, jazz poetics and who, also, not too surprisingly, relating to our journey into an entire eternal circuitry of the mortal coil, created a hallucinatory, shrouded visionary, deathwatch character in his allegorical novel entitled *Doctor Sax*.

In other words: two Jacks who were fifty years apart inspired an American vernacular connected to a nonlinear phrasing in storytelling, arguably, converting the sound of, at the very least, narrative novels and designating the demand of "give me immortality or give me death" forever. However, although, a main incentive, here, in examining an encroaching of my own mortality, by recently scanning the words of both London and Kerouac, has, always, been a need to decompress, mainly, inspired by my suspicion that both of their lead characters were never going to last past Chapter 3.

As an additional true fact (redundantly speaking) being my opinion that both of their protagonists, always, appeared to be living phantoms, moving towards an endgame very similar to the realm of aging in which we, lately, find ourselves as literary contributors—an endangered brood emanating from an apolitical sub-culture—totally, identifying it as (for lack of a better more colorful euphemism) Death!

ON WRITING AND DYING, AND DYING TO WRITE

GARY YOUNG

FOR THE PAST twenty years, I have taught creative writing at a university, and as a consequence, I spend my days with young people. I know their slang, I know their music, and I feel young myself when I'm with them, as if by some kind of sweet osmosis I can take on their vitality and their passion. That bubble was broken recently when a student brought an old book of mine into class. The book was passed around, and one charming young woman stared at the author's photo on the back cover, glanced over at me, and said, "You looked just like you do now, only healthy."

The sickness she so astutely diagnosed and had no restraint in verbalizing is age. I have a bad case. I am almost 70, and as much as I would like to think that proximity to the young somehow keeps me youthful, a mirror and my aching knees are enough to remind me of the truth: I am old, and getting older.

In many ways my mother prepared me for this eventuality. From the time I was a child she called me her "little man," and by the time I was a teenager, I had taken on the duties and the responsibilities of an adult. While she languished in bed, debilitated by depression, I shopped for groceries, made dinner for my siblings, and spent my evenings at the laundromat washing clothes while I did my homework. Poetry was my lifeline during those years. I haunted the library, and roamed the Poetry section, gobbling up everything from the Romantics to the Beats. I started writing poetry myself, and carried my precious manuscripts in an old briefcase, which I would open at my desk or on a bench at the park, where I'd scribble my verses, and dream about being a real poet.

I studied poetry in college, received an MFA, published poems in journals and anthologies, and was waiting impatiently for my first book to be released when I was struck down with a level-4 melanoma. I wasn't yet 30. I endured a catastrophic surgery, was told I had little chance of survival, and was encouraged to put my things in order. If I was dying, I knew how I wanted to spend my final days. I moved to a little cabin in the Santa Cruz Mountains, continued to write poems, and waited to die. I have lived in that little cabin for over forty years. My cancer has returned more than once, and I have spent my adult life accepting that the end is surely near.

Cancer appears only rarely in my poems, but the evanescence of life and the inevitability of death are recurring themes. I feel as if I have carried my own death with me like a smooth stone cradled in my pocket. Sometimes I rub it for comfort.

A young poet responding to a fatal disease is romantic, gallant, and even sexy. An old poet responding to disease or frailty is just another literary elder complaining about the inevitable. But what old poets know, and what I was lucky enough to learn at an early age, is that death is always with us. It is waiting in the bus when we step off a curb; waiting in the blood test, and in the bad batch of drugs; waiting in our sleep; waiting to explode like fireworks in our brains.

The great and sorrowful gift of age is to feel death in our bodies, and to see death in those we love. I have lived with the surety of my own death for as long as I can remember. I have held hands with the dying, mourned parents, children, lovers, and friends. I am sick with age, and eventually, I will die of it. In the meantime, I will do what I did while I waited to die when I was young: I will keep writing, and pray that the writing will keep me alive.

IN WHICH I GET VERY SICK, AM RESCUED BY DREW CAREY, THEN HAVE A ONE-ON-ONE WITH THE GRIM REAPER HIMSELF

RON KOERTGE

DEATH IS USUALLY a he, and he has lots of aliases: *Thanatos, San La Muerte, Shinigami*, or maybe just one of the Chinese Ghost Kings. Different costumes but basically the same concept. He's something all of us have to deal with at some point, whether he's clad in a tattered cloak, a fashionable hoodie, or something more culturally sensitive. No matter what he's wearing, we know who he is and what's on his mind.

Not long ago, I certainly knew who he was and I was afraid that I was on his mind. When I was 75, some out-patient surgery went wrong. Inside of forty-eight hours, sepsis led to septic shock and ER doctors shouting for assistance. Without antibiotics, I wouldn't be writing this.

Clearly I survived but was knocked, as they used to say, for a loop. I was out of danger but also out of everything else: ambition, energy, desire. I slept a lot, gathering enough vitality to see my acupuncturist and sleep on her table. Books fell out of my hands as I tried to read. Soup spoons clattered to the floor as I nearly dozed off at lunch.

I couldn't go out. I didn't want to go out. I wanted only to watch *The Price Is Right*. Drew Carey—the amiable and sympathetic host of the show—was Death's opposite. Death's bespectacled foe. And his audience—ardent and fervent—Drew's troops.

While my life force was reduced to the status of a flickering pilot light,

Drew's audience wanted to guess the price of things so much they almost combusted. They whooped and shrieked and applauded and jumped up and down. They cheered the chosen contestants and lamented the overlooked.

I propped myself up on the couch every weekday at 11 a.m. and fed off their energy. By the time the show was over, I'd siphoned off enough exuberance to walk all the way to the kitchen.

Once I could sit up and stay awake for more than twenty-two minutes, I started back to work as a registered smarty pants—writing poems and making fun of AARP's advertisements for bathtubs with doors and heated lounge chairs with settings from Nap-to-Coma.

My wife and my friends were glad to see me back at the computer because I am no fun to be with when, even at my best, I'm not writing. And I'd been nowhere near at my best.

Guess what? Death wasn't through with me. He dropped by most nights. The dreams were rarely nightmares. They were, in fact, embarrassingly lackluster and by-the-book. But there he was in the dream-world as I looked for my car or took a test I wasn't prepared for or walked naked up the aisle of Holy Family church as everyone tittered and stared. He didn't whisper the answer to question #23 or find my Toyota or offer me his cloak, but he was there. Not threatening, not baleful. Just there. His face hidden, as usual. Sometimes the scythe lay over his shoulder. Sometimes he'd lean on it like a weary farmer.

I got used to him hanging around. He struck me as solitary. An outcast, really. A pariah. Nobody wants death at their table. Nobody picks him for their team.

I felt for him, perhaps because I'd been isolated while various fevers lit up the landscape of my body. Life then seemed to go on completely without me. Like Death, I was marginalized. Left out. Unloved. So in the first poem I wrote about him, I took care of that.

Death Takes a Shower

Slips into jeans and a T-shirt.
Opens a cold beer.

There's golf on TV. His wife watches
with him, they talk about the kids

who are at school till 3:00. Plenty
of time she says, "If you want to,
sweetie."

He does. It's a lonely business.
He's on the road a lot and misses
her.

Afterwards, she naps. He checks his
watch. Forty-five minutes before
the yellow school bus drops off the girls.

He goes into his office and works
from home for a while.

Death became someone with a truly terrible job and always alone. But I
took care of that. I know what projection is and I'm sure I wanted to come home
to my old self, too—trips to the races, dinners with friends, sex in the afternoon.

Did that poem help? Yes and no. Death was still in the margins of my
dreams, but I wasn't afraid anymore. Well, not that afraid. But I wondered
what he wanted. More, probably. Isn't that what we all want?

Hillary Mantel, author of *Wolf Hall* and *Bring Up the Bodies*, told an NPR
interviewer that she talks to her characters. She puts them in a chair and interrogates
them. So I invited Death in. He propped his scythe in the corner. He sat and
arranged his cloak. He told me what he wanted. I was right. He wanted more.

Mr. Death

picks up his briefcase and heads for the front door.
His wife is there with a lunch box and a muffler.
"It's cold," she says, "stay warm. How long are you
gone for this time?" "Not too bad," he says. "Three
days, probably. I'll be at the Holiday Inn."

"There's a tuna salad sandwich and soup in the thermos.
Eat the tuna first. There's mayo in it. And for

breakfast at the buffet, no sausages, okay?
Eat something with fiber. Just remember how
many people are waiting for you."

"I know," says Death, "they're old and sick,
which is fine. It's the young ones that kind
of break my heart."

"Don't think about them, sweetie. Have you
got a book? There's always something on TV
if you can't sleep. Or just call me, okay?"

He kisses his wife goody-bye, walks to his car
and starts it. He lets it run for a minute or two.
He's always cold. The heater helps a little,
but not enough. Nothing is enough. Still,
he turns it to High, waves to his wife,
and pulls away from the curb.

That seemed to do the trick. More. More affection and understanding
from his wife. More sympathy with his lot in, ironically, life. More. More.
More. More from me, too. For weeks I read that poem out loud every morning.
In a way, every day I sent him off on his ghastly errands.

Little by little he stepped into the shadows again. Maybe having coffee
with his best friend—Taxes.

I don't think about him much these days. I feel pretty well. I'm reasonably
productive. I entertain my friends. But I haven't forgotten. When I read about
thousands dying, I remember Death's relentless reaping and my blood runs
cold. But then I imagine him weary and misunderstood hurrying home. A
living room lit by a fire. A door he opens with a bony hand and then this:

Death's Dog

When he hears the car door
slam, he picks up that red

ball and wags his entire behind.
Death says, "Who's a good boy?"

Then changes into some old clothes
and out to the back yard they go.

Blackie will chase the ball
until he's exhausted, then keel

over, let his tongue dangle,
and play dead. It's the only

trick he knows but it's his
owner's favorite.

AGING IN THREE PARTS

NILS PETERSON

PART ONE: ON WINDING THE CLOCK

As long as there is one upright man, as long as there is one
compassionate woman, the contagion may spread and the scene
is not desolate. Hope is the thing that is left to us, in a bad time.
I shall get up Sunday morning and wind the clock, as a
contribution to order and steadfastness.

—E.B. White

I LOVED THIS SENTENCE when I first read it, "I shall get up Sunday morning and wind the clock, as a contribution to order and steadfastness," but the more I thought about it last night at two in the morning, the sadder I became.

Nobody winds their clock anymore except in antique shops. Wrist watches either. They're run, if you have one, by battery. Your physical connection with the world of time, once a daily responsibility, is now a once a year connection with someone who changes batteries. I need to except those watches that get their motion from the swinging of your arm as you go about your day. But that removes the consciousness of winding as a contribution to "order and steadfastness." The modern equivalent is "Make sure you put your iWatch on the charger."

What a wonder the watch was, an appropriate gift for high school graduation, something that you needed to care for, and, yes, wind. And the seven day mantel clock, it measured the week as well ticking the minutes and bonging the hours. And then the grandfather clock. My father's friend Eric Sporre made one out of scraps of wood at a time when he was out of work in the Depression. It was beautiful, painted a Swedish blue, and had a little window where you could watch the brass pendulum do its work and a little door to open to wind the spring. Then there was the enormous one in the hallway of the great house of the rich people my father worked for as a chauffeur, also during the Depression. I would see it at least every Christmas when we went on Christmas Eve for the servants' presents. It had a round dial on top with a moving sun and moon, maybe zodiacal signs, and below a panel with a ship going up and down on waves maybe meant to be the waves of time. One could believe in time then and one's responsibility to be in tune with it. "In tune," yes, it was a kind of music. Now I think of the insistence of the metronome, though it too now is an app on a phone instead of a wand you would wind before you started your piano practice.

I'm in my 80s. A few years ago I wrote, "There are fewer and fewer/ native speakers of one's born language. You learn to live with translations." Watch-winding now needs a translation.

I want to end with a quotation from an essay by William Maxwell called "Nearing Ninety." He's been asked if he's still writing. He replies, "Nothing very much," then confesses to us that it is, "The truth but not the whole truth." He goes on to say, "I still like making sentences." He ends with this little paragraph, "Every now and then, in my waking moments, and especially when I'm in the country, I stand and look hard at everything."

I guess that's what I want to do too as I sidle towards 90, "look hard at everything" and make sentences, though I may take a moment to wind my high school graduation watch wherever it may be.

PART TWO: CROW'S NEST

Been haunted by the image of a crow's nest lately, the one on top of the tallest mast of an old sailing ship, and thinking about the first time one climbed up to it, maybe you're 12 or 13, the bosun's sent you aloft, rope ladder after rope ladder, up and up, and soon you're 150 feet up on a swaying perch looking down at a swaying sea.

Isn't this like aging? One climbs up a swaying rope ladder of year after year and all of a sudden you're 86 swaying above a sea of years.

I come to the image by way of *Treasure Island*, actually a poem by Seamus Heaney I like a lot that refers to *Treasure Island*. Here is the stanza I'm thinking of now, the final stanza of "In the Attic":

> As I age and blank on names,
> As my uncertainty on stairs
> Is more and more the lightheadedness
>
> Of a cabin boy's first time on the rigging,
> As the memorable bottoms out
> Into the irretrievable....

Yes, yes, "uncertainty on stairs" and "As the memorable bottoms out/ Into the irretrievable...."

In the poem, he's standing in the attic of his old childhood house and looks out of the window at a birch tree, planted as a sapling, when Memory brings the ghost of his grandfather who brings a ghost of *Treasure Island*, and the speaker finds himself for a moment both young and old:

> A birch tree planted twenty years ago
> Comes between the Irish Sea and me
> At the attic skylight, a man marooned
>
> In his own loft, a boy
> Shipshaped in the crow's nest of a life . . .

At a certain age, everything has a touch of elegy. It is not depressing, just a sense of where the world is and where you are in it. And memory, that old friend, moves from the neighborhood into a senior residence and visits you when it can, leaving me this morning feeling like

> . . . a boy
> Shipshaped in the crow's nest of a life.

PART THREE: AGING

I'm not a big fan of David Brooks, but I found this bit in one of his columns that has stayed with me: "Each close friend you have brings out a version of yourself that you could not bring out on your own. When your close friend dies, you are not only losing the friend, you are losing the version of your personality that he or she elicited."

It made me realize how much I miss Steve, my good friend who died not long ago, and not only how I miss Steve, but I miss the man I was when I was with Steve. We would have lunch together once or twice a month. The talk was always good. It was about everything, *The World, The Flesh, and Father Smith.* That's the title of an old novel that of all my friends Steve would have been the most likely to remember and realize why it came to mind just now.

I have other friends that I am almost the same as I was with Steve, but it is almost. So, I mourn the loss of Steve, and I mourn the loss of the Nils who would have lunch with Steve.

And then I read a poem by W.S. Merwin, a favorite poet of mine. He refers to the old song "In the Gloaming," and I wonder how many people are left who would catch the reference. I remember my mother playing it on the upright piano which was maybe the next thing my father bought for her after a bed, a table, and a chair, "In the gloaming, oh, my darling when the lights are dim and low...." I hum the tune as I type.

I say in one of my poems that:

> There are fewer and fewer
> native speakers of one's born language.
>
> You learn to live with translations.

So, age whittles us away, shaving by shaving, as loved ones, friends, and the shared bits of ordinary life fall and we stand alone before the immensity of what is to come.

LATE LIFE CREATIVITY: A PERSONAL JOURNEY

MARTIN LINDAUER

"YOU CAN'T TEACH an old dog new tricks" is an adage that competes with "You're never too old to learn." Can we say the same about creativity? Does it disappear with old age? Continue? Fade? Change? Can it emerge late in life?

At age 30, with a new PhD in psychology, I was fairly well acquainted with the scientific literature on creativity. The evidence generally indicated that noteworthy achievements of the highest order occurred largely in youth, subsided in early adulthood, and faltered if not disappeared by middle age or so. Thus, the best predictor of adult creativity was youthful achievement, not modest success and certainly not mediocre efforts.

There were exceptions, though. The early promise of child prodigies faded and disappeared as they grew older. Goya, Matisse, and Titian maintained a high level of creativity into their 60s and later. Late life creativity continued for Martha Graham and Stravinsky. Longstanding accomplishments outside of the arts include Galileo (among scientists), Churchill (statesmen), and Oliver Wendell Holmes (jurists). "Late-bloomers," like Grandma Moses, displayed new and unexpected creativity late in life.

Of special interest are creative artists with an established reputation who developed an "old age style." A marked shift in their later years characterizes the work of Monet, Verdi, and G. B. Shaw. However, unexpected and often idiosyncratic changes in old age were often interpreted as a decline in creativity, the result of pathological or biological factors, such as the loss of eyesight or waning physic strength. The creative achievements after age 65 of some were belatedly recognized many years after their deaths.

Aside from the exceptions, experts maintained in the main, that, with age ideas become stagnant; earlier efforts are repeated; old themes are reworked; and prosaic if not predictable works are produced, reflecting a nostalgic harking back to earlier contributions.

Investigators of creativity have therefore emphasized the priority of early markers in identifying creativity. Thus, discussions and studies of creativity emphasized youthful exemplars. Hence, there is a great deal of interest ("What might have been?") in creative people who died young: Mozart, Chopin, Schubert, and Mendelssohn in music; and Van Gogh, Correggio, Raphael, and Toulouse-Lautrec among painters.

In light of the preponderance of evidence, outlined above, I grudgingly acknowledged the sad fact that early indicators of creativity had not appeared in me—yet. But I was hopeful, since my chronological age was not equivalent to my "occupational age." I had spent two years in the Army after college, a year abroad in my second year of graduate school and I'd held a part-time teaching job while pursuing an advanced degree. As a result, it had taken me almost ten years to receive my doctorate. Subtracting the time spent on non-academic activities from my current age I estimated that I still had a few years' grace before I reached the critical middle years. According to most studies that might be when my star (finally) ascended.

By the time I celebrated my 40th birthday, though, I could no longer postpone facing the truth. The absence of youthful creative achievements had indeed foretold my future. I finally accepted reality: I was not destined to become one of the movers and shakers of my field. Reluctantly, but realistically, I gave up any lofty aspirations (or were they pretensions?) of fulfilling an unexpressed creative potential. I resigned myself to remaining a journeyman, one of the many "laborers in the field." I would have to be content, I decided, with producing competent work in a small corner of a specialized area of some sub-field. The most I could hope for was modest recognition among a small number of my peers who worked in the same narrow specialty as I did.

In my 50s, though, I began to wonder if more modest forms of late-life creativity might emerge among those who, like me, were not among the great, famous, and eminent, neither a prize- nor award- winner. Thus, I turned to fulfilling the adage (adapted): those who can, do; those who can't, write a book. I published *Aging, Creativity, and Art.*

No surprise, the book presented my research on tracking the accomplishments of hundreds of historical painters who lived to at least 80; surveying the published views of art historians on late art and aging artists; recording the results of questionnaires on late-life creativity completed by aging contemporary artists; tallying undergraduates and senior citizens' preferences for the art of young and old artists; and obtaining self-reports by 20- to 80-year-olds on their participation, interest, and attitudes towards the arts and arts-related activities.

The 300 pages of tightly reasoned and data-filled text—together with the more than a dozen tables and graphs, numerous statistical footnotes, nearly a hundred bibliographic endnotes, many pages of references, and several appendices—made the case for possible alternative trajectories of late-life creative development. My goal (or hope) was to temper the near universal belief in the early surge of creativity, its eventual decline, and predictable loss in late life.

The book emphasized objective, empirical, research-oriented, and quantitative approaches. Little attention was paid to anecdotal, private, and subjective contributions or introspective accounts, informal testimonies, epiphanies, astute revelations, penetrating conjectures, shrewd analyses, credible quotations, and convincing rhetoric. Speculative approaches, while adding another way to understand late-life creativity, mainly served as suggestive leads for further research of a more rigorous sort.

As a break from my academic labors, the laboratory, professional journals, and the library's stacks, I took a watercolor class. Near the end of the course, I experienced a personal insight about the creative process.

It began when I complained to the instructor about the amateurish quality of my paintings. She replied, "Don't compare yourself to what others do but to the work you did when you first began."

Her remark, albeit hardly scientific, suggested another way, simple yet reasonable, of evaluating late-life accomplishments. I began to rethink the evidence I had marshaled on late-life creativity and the dispiriting conclusion I had come to in evaluating my professional record. My art instructor was telling me that current accomplishments are not the sole criterion for self-appraisal. Rather, what counts are the changes that occurred over a semester—or a lifetime. Thus, comparing current efforts to earlier ones was another means for discerning the course of creativity.

Armed with this insight I considered a number of other possible indicators of late-life creativity, the small-c rather than big-C kind, the latter achieved by Nobel Prize winners and the like. Small-c examples of late-life creativity might be manifested by changing one's occupation, starting a new career, and moving into a different field of endeavor. For scholars, other options were exploring a new field, writing reviews, and critiquing the work of others. Researchers could advise and mentor a younger generation of scientists. Academics, more broadly, could follow unfamiliar lines of inquiry. As for the aging in general, the non-professionals, small-c creativity might be illustrated by setting new goals or redirecting old ones; practicing other modes of thinking, such as the reflective and philosophical; becoming more open to experience, to others, to life around you; and writing a memoir, perhaps on the lessons learned over a lifetime.

Additional creative outlets in old age include searching within one's self for submerged talents; recharging latent interests; pursuing youthful dreams; seeking spiritual refreshment; engaging in volunteer activities; improving the lives of those less fortunate; showing greater tolerance and more understanding of others as well as one's self; and reevaluating earlier failures and preoccupations as a step towards establishing new pursuits.

As I move through the eighth decade of my life I am more optimistic than I was at age 30 about the creative potential of old age.

KNOCKING ON DEATH'S DOOR (WHILE WRITING ABOUT IT)

ANDREW MERTON

ON THURSDAY, May 17, 1962, six days after my 18th birthday, my father died of a heart attack. He was 48. It was, and remains, the worst day of my life.

In the more than half-century that has followed I have lived through many deaths, ranging from family members and close friends to statesmen and women, athletes and celebrities I have admired. Each brings its own keen sense of loss. Each one hurts. Each diminishes me. (Toni Morrison, where are you when we need you?)

About my own impending death, I feel differently. After all, I will not be around to grieve and mourn me.

It's coming, of course. It's implied in the second word of my title, professor emeritus. The formal definition of emeritus is "honorably discharged," but what it means is, on his way out. When a professor dies we are shocked and saddened. When a professor emeritus dies we are not shocked.

So, it's coming. What will it be like?

I wrote the following poem, first published in the *Alaska Quarterly Review*, in 2010, at age 65:

Your Date with Death

starts with low expectations.
You don't even bother to shave.
Well, forget what you've heard about her.

She's Wendy, your high school sweetheart,
still eighteen, dressed in white.
(How could you have dumped her?)

She takes your hand
and you think peaches, waterfalls,
the smell of suntan lotion

on bare shoulders.
Now you can finally dance—
not the tango you once craved,

but a mannered waltz
in a mirrored ballroom,
ending with a curtsy and a bow.

Later, at her door, she thanks you.
Feeling shy, you ask,
What's it like, being Death?

On good nights, she says,
it's like this,
and she kisses you hard.

In this rendition Death (and it is very much my own death I'm fantasizing about here) is not the traditional cloaked, scythe-wielding, skeletal fellow, but a young, attractive girl/woman, still in her teens.

It is not that I look forward to death. In my mid-70s, despite a bit of arthritis here and some stenosis there, I am reasonably healthy. I avoid fried foods, drink only in moderation (the fact that my beloved single malts are expensive helps with this) and, in decent weather, I take long walks, during which I do much fruitful revising.

Most days, I enjoy being alive. I enjoy writing, reading, concerts, movies, traveling with my wife, the company of friends and family, most especially my grandson, age 3.

On the other hand, there are occasional days, weeks, even months, when I think I might as well be dead. I suffer from (or, to employ the currently fashionable euphemism, live with) bipolar 2, a mental illness featuring occasional manic episodes scattered among prolonged periods of deep depression. At the bottom of the worst of these troughs, death can seem welcoming, a relief, a remedy. I admit to one ill-considered and half-assed suicide attempt at age 30. Following my second divorce, I chased down a bottle of Quaaludes with some cheap whiskey and woke up 36 hours later. Eventually I underwent electroconvulsive therapy, or ECT, or shock treatment; it may well have saved my life. (Like the prospect of my own death, my struggles with mental illness have provided a rich trove of writing material; I've published poems and essays on depression, bipolarity, and ECT.)

There were other near misses—car crashes in 1968 and 1971, a college career as a bass player in a rock band the members of which habitually drove drunk—and a problematic issue of heredity: my father had his first heart attack at 41, and longevity has never been an attribute of the genetic makeup of his side of my family. It would be easy to say that I'm living on borrowed time, although I find that concept flawed; how in the world is one supposed to pay off the loan?

In any case, I'm glad I have survived into my 70s. Through it all, I have kept writing, often dealing, directly or indirectly, with the nature, and inevitability, of death.

Of course it is impossible to imagine being dead. Imagination requires awareness, something missing in death. Much as I would like to imagine dying and death as a matter of walking off a baseball diamond into a cornfield, as in *Field of Dreams*, I do not believe in an afterlife. I assume that death equals nonexistence. How to imagine that? The best I can do is to consider general anesthesia, a loss of consciousness far more profound than simple sleep. In 2018 I underwent a surgical procedure during which I was put under for approximately 90 minutes. The last thing I remember is starting the countdown from ten, as the anesthesiologist had suggested. I might have gotten as far as seven. After that, nothing. No sensations, no memory. No imagination either, nothing until afterward—the only difference between death and anesthesia being that with the latter, there is an afterward.

I do not find the certainty of this coming nothingness frightening. Each of us has an appointment in Samarra. (In the 1933 Somerset Maugham retelling of this story, incidentally, Death is female.) For most of us, excluding the likes of condemned prisoners and people in the final stages of terminal diseases, the only questions are when, where, how.

There is a passage from Annie Dillard's 1982 essay "Total Eclipse," in which Dillard and her husband Gary traveled to the Yakima Valley in central Washington to observe one, that stays with me. As Dillard watched the moon blot out the sun, she writes, Gary ". . . smiled as if he saw me; the stringy crinkles around his eyes moved. The sight of him, familiar and wrong, was something I was remembering from centuries hence, from the other side of death: Yes, that is the way he used to look, when we were living. When it was our generation's turn to be alive."

Mine is among the generations whose turn it is now to be alive. Our only turn. For each one of us the duration is unknown, but even under the best of circumstances I'm at least three-quarters done. Still, I continue to write, although at nowhere near the pace or output of even fifteen years ago.

I once had a brilliant MFA student who published several stories while still in school. A few years later she wrote to me that she had decided to stop writing, and to devote her life to other things. "It's such a relief!" she said. Some great writers—most recently, perhaps, the incandescent Alice Munro, after winning the Nobel Prize for literature in 2013, at the age of 82—announce that they will no longer write. I can imagine that happening to me, but not yet.

Let me be clear: dying, as opposed to death, scares the hell out of me. I have seen bad deaths. When it comes down to it, I would prefer to go via physician-assisted death, and may be willing to move to one of the nine states in which the practice is currently legal and regulated.

But that seems off the subject.

As for death itself? Although I am in no hurry, I am at peace with the prospect. And, like any other transition, it is a subject worth writing about. In addition to fantasies like "Your Date with Death" and "Autopsy" (about my own), there are poems about my suicide attempt and my father's death, as well as about my mother's death at 78, my sister's, at 64, and of a pilot, age unknown, of a small plane in the jungles of Peru. While all of them are dark, none, I think, are gloomy, hopeless. I'll close with one of my more recent efforts regarding the hovering certainty of my own demise:

Early Winter Nor'easter

Your body's a ramshackle farmhouse,
paint peeling, sills rotting,
roof leaking;

still, you'll survive this blizzard,
and maybe even the next,
already forming off the coast.

Meanwhile, inside,
a grizzled hound
of uncertain pedigree,

circles the green braided rug
in front of the fire,
looking for a place to settle.

AFTER THE FINAL NO, THERE COMES A YES

ELENA KARINA BYRNE

The Well Dressed Man with a Beard

After the final no there comes a yes
And on that yes the future world depends.
No was the night. Yes is this present sun.
If the rejected things, the things denied,
Slid over the western cataract, yet one,
One only, one thing that was firm, even
No greater than a cricket's horn, no more
Than a thought to be rehearsed all day, a speech
Of the self that must sustain itself on speech,
One thing remaining, infallible, would be
Enough. Ah! douce campagna of that thing!
Ah! douce campagna, honey in the heart,
Green in the body, out of a petty phrase,
Out of a thing believed, a thing affirmed:
The form on the pillow humming while one sleeps,
The aureole above the humming house . . .
It can never be satisfied, the mind, never.

—Wallace Stevens

THE CHOICE TO BE A WRITER is an incident, a point of departure that requires the force of memory's exigency to live. Catherine Malbou recounted Spinoza's story of seventeenth-century poet named Góngora; before death, Góngora lost his memory and hence, a radical, essential part of his personality. In the *Ontology of the Accident*, Malbou gives all of us a reason to fear something beyond memory loss: fear of self-creation through our writing. "The writer who no longer remembers his own books, who no longer remembers himself, is dead without being dead." So, it might also be fair to say that language is an entity capable of immortality, that corruptible brain-tool that stands between life and death. Can it be adequately equipped to keep up with our brain's high-speed hemispheric, Dante-like terza rima-tirade between fire and ice? Hyperbole sings back: Art saves lives, writing saved mine.

Of course, everything living has in its DNA a survival code. Humans are divined and divided by language; we *live and die by the sword* held up by the gospel-influence of language and image. History reminds us that each language is unique and adapts with each body politics' culture: Words die or are adopted, re-translated, caught inside the mouth of youth commerce. Is the insistence on youth culture the new eugenics? I go back to being 14 years old when I decided to be a poet, an accident, yet also, not an accident. A fresh teenager's atopia to being told what to do—a teen looking for some personalized art of persuasion, a platform for recognition and belonging . . . looking for that sword with which to battle mortality.

What can survive the politics of a culture? Language is a live animal that lives inside of us. However, many regional language dialects, like select species of Darwin's animals, die. The "living us and the dead us" (Dorothea Lasky, *Animal*) decree what comes next. Writers, filmmakers, photographers, musicians, and artists contribute to the ever-evolving linguistic platform. *Nice going!* The sarcastic intonation use of this phrase dredges up an original meaning. In 1290, *nice* meant something altogether different (*foolish and stupid!*) from what it means now. Chaucer used it in a way to mean lascivious, which makes me cringe seeing some drunken character in a film slur the word *very slowly* as he sees a young beauty walk by. Hitch your wagon to the next halfwit phrase a commercial or politician bleeds from the mouth—see what happens.

Language can begin in intimacy and end in remoteness; it obfuscates as easily as it clarifies. In other words, poetry for example, as a creative material, might as well be a massive lump of clay in our hands. What happens when we override the brain's signals? Metaphysical angst-artist Chris Burden asked a "friend" to shoot him in front of a gallery audience in 1971; in another performance piece, embodying his own metaphor, he crawls across broken glass until the hands and feet of the audience hurt. The viewer is held hostage, and, as a result, there's an ambush made on the thought process. Burden, as a performer, invites us to be uncomfortable, participatory witnesses, complicit voyeurs. Inevitably, that compelling discomfort invites us to come in closer to and risk our own death. William Gass, in his inexorable book *On Being Blue: A Philosophical Inquiry*, pairs concepts of longing and melancholy in a sweet abstract Rorschach test of creative conjecture: "The blue we bathe in is the blue we breathe. The blue we breathe, I fear, is what we want from life and only find it in fiction. For the voyeur, fiction is what's called going all the way." Ah, the sweet persuasions of fiction. If you love what language can do almost as much as you love what the body can do, then you must be an aging writer who wants to *tell* herself that she is still looking for intimacy, still very alive!

Tell once meant to count—count what, one wonders. For the sake of this argument, let's say to count our lives in words, minute by day, hour by year, second by inhale syllable-breath, and light, mid-flight. Now, language and the human mind are at each other's *beck and call*, at each other's mercy, *never satisfied*. A turn of phrase can *make or break* a deal, draw in a crowd, create a love for a product, or stir up hate for a type of people, elect a dummy candidate, and in private, keep tabs on our tethered planet, the heart. Predecessor-experts say that language means to be one of the tools that separate us from other animals, providing logic and therefore keeping us civilized. But our civilization is not so civilized and does not keep us "upright," or human, i.e., intelligent and therefore compassionate-aware, empathic and tolerant of the infinite other diverse humans on this planet. Unfortunately, it won't keep us from killing each other, protect us from our own mortality.

We are inextricably bound to time, and the body's clock—the interplay-entanglement displays of transfiguration on the dramatic survival stage of life. Everything life and everything language are about such measurements, about action and inaction, grammar's future imperfect: *going* . . . yet, *going* implies an act of departure: someone leaving; our health, our looks departing, pieces of our memory, and so on. But what *comes* to mind, what comes to us via language's ongoing realm of the everlasting, can be equally narrowed down to a list of subject's heartbeat-paired set of words like *life* & *death*. Bill Bryson, in his latest book, *The Body: A Guide for Occupants*, paints a nuanced picture of the heart of the matter in the differing lifestyles and bodies of select creatures: "An elephant's heart beats just thirty times a minute, a human's sixty, a cow's between fifty and eighty, but a mouse beats six-hundred times a minute–ten times a second. Just to survive, the mouse must eat 50 percent of its own body weight."

I don't presume we can think about sex, food, and death that fast, but *in one fell swoop*, in one breath, our hungry brains can create something exciting and new out of the three. Yet, language, that sixth sense, another body part, can control perception and instigate change. Can the body of language transform the body like an octopus? Stand on your head and rub someone else's tummy. Surprise yourself. The corporate money-bag man, Steve Wynn, who, while revitalizing Las Vegas, the adult Disneyland, declared, "if you don't reinvent, you die." Did he put his *skin in the game*? As an aging author, increasingly, I find that writing has to become conscience. It has to be an act of translation for others. Skin in the game means taking risks, letting go of ego, riding out the waves . . . and reinventing. Here, language redefines immortality where thinking slows downs or speeds up the liminal consciousness as it unites joy and grief––what enables me to believe in poetry's relative beauty. So, maybe I'm sometimes rushing toward ground zero when I write or paint, but you can bet I will show attentive care when I engage in sex acts with my lover or step outside into nature, aware of the uneven ground beneath my feet. The once youth favorite dark subject matters of nascent writing have now been exchanged for something new. Further complicating this ever-changing age-equation, I might then say that I no longer take Dostoyevsky's anonymous *Underground* "pleasure of despair" with me home at night. I *happen* to be a happy person who sometimes is in love with discovering the beauty that survives from darkness.

Any discourse we fumbling poets have with the neverlands, netherworlds of heaven, paradise, purgatory, with nirvana, hell, and the beyond, with an imagined resting-place, Olympus, with final silence, well . . . . The faith-based story-history-nutshells either can be found stuffed inside the mouth of some squirrel as he grapples up a tree or found buried in autumn's leaf-mulch field by the eager mountain jay. Miguel de Unamuno insisted that "nothing is lost, nothing wholly passes away, for in some way or another everything is

perpetuated; and everything, after passing through time, returns to eternity."
(*Tragic Sense of Life*) Whether we believe in an "eternity" or not, we know
everything to do with human behaviors *is perpetuated*. *How* those things are
perpetuated fascinates me. From a writer's standpoint, it's all about how we
approach the same handful of subjects, repeatedly, with inexhaustible, perverse
enthusiasm, desire, and sense of belonging to know and re-know our world.
This desire brings us back to the movie theater, back to a new canvas, back to
the writer's pages, and is everything to do with being alive. Dorothy Lasky's
answer to *what does love care about* might equally be true for the art of writing:
"Love is all about what it means to need."

Like language or love, death can never be *solved*. Death, a noun, turns on
the imagination until it becomes an active verb. As final as that seems, deaths,
close to us, stay alive in our minds; every death there loiters, plays itself out
over and over. Death acts in ultimate rebellion to personal knowledge. Death
is the master of persona, of the mirror. Cocteau's mirror! In *Orpheus*, Cocteau
says life is merely a long death, the reason why he created that pain-induced
love triangle between the struggling writer Orpheus, his married love Eurydice,
and the new, never-to-be ignored seductress, Death. But the personified Death
must be genderless! If we are in-vertigo-love with Death, then I imagine our
love triangle to be made up of a triad/triptych of selves: the original animal self
we feel, the projected self that others see, and death as one's subsumed self, that
omniscient parent (the writer) who will always weave together her perilous rope
bridge for all to cross. As death imparts a metonymic proxy for life, another
language's *la petite mort* appears on the written page of individual happiness.

When asked why I am a writer, I reply: *Because my parents were artists.*
They gave me double sight, taught me how to see, allowed me to speak in
images, and to think with my body. My parents died but their memory and
artworks did not. My mother and father remain alive inside their death, inside
of me; their artworks exist. My parents' mingling body of ashes swim the
ocean and memory's family of oceans. Once gone, our parents who became
part of us, become phantom limbs. I feel my mother, remember her with a
physiological precision, and so am always grateful when she comes "alive" in
my thinking and, more so, in my dreams. But to see yourself through the
lexicon, you may have to go back to Shakespeare in order to be able to reply,
"I'm down with that." Terrance Hayes, in his *Lit Hub* interview said, "I'm
interested in Shakespeare, but especially how Shakespeare is in conversation

with *Scooby-Doo* or *The Walking Dead.*" Ghosts of language too, contain this inherent ambiguity. I recall my first professor, Thomas Lux, then still very alive, gesturing his two fingers and thumb toward the ceiling as he read to us out loud as he breathed poetry's blood-fire back into the class, telling the 18-year-old student, "Once you write the poem, it no longer belongs to you." Yes, Thomas: No more preciousness, *my precious!* Let it go to where it belongs: into the salty language seas, back into the muddy body earth.

Imagine the character Harold (*Harold and Maude*) trying out his many deaths, with a banjo, dancing-out re-birth on the film's green cliff end. Death and grief certainly taught me patience; what else requires incredible patience? (Patience equals care, equals thinking's measurement of time.) Writing. Aging. Publishing. Lovemaking. Child-rearing. Art. Aging. Yes, I repeat aging because it houses both permanence and impermanence. After all, the body's aging is always self-perpetuating, always in motion; age never stops its yammering vigil by our side until we do. Well, I take that back: we never really "stop" either, since we become semi-inert, organic monuments of instant decay after death. If language lives by constant motion like body and mind, then our individualized uses of language figure as separate divagations to make up one imperfect time-hinge.

What keeps on living after the other dies, brain or heart? We are told a good love relationship can physically alter how long you live, therefore transforming health, even your DNA. I wonder if that could include a good relationship with our art. Writing, tied to Eros and her erotic impulse, engages all the senses. The physiology of the phrases cannot be separated from their meaning. In the same way, I cannot imagine true intelligence without compassion; not imagine being physically separated from the outside world as we have been during COVID. Do you think creative logic, for the poet, the filmmaker, will quell our panic for survival, alter this disquieted picture? Despite possessing some corporeal and intellectual command over my writing, I know it commands me.

The more I write and the more I know, the marginally more anxious I feel. I'm anxious for what will and must come next, from inside this medicinal wonder and poison of our art. Like Kierkegaard's dystopic anxiety, *the dizziness of freedom, I* want new language-play only found in research. I want to follow the counterintuitive, challenge myself. This physiological map that charts a course toward living . . . as I say this, I see bright stone fruits falling around me in the heat, surrounded by morning's slick grass as a fuss of black ants carry their sweet from the wet, sticky flesh, back home, the heart, the start of it all. I want to comb my hair between birch limbs, let the sea's longing take my weight from me; I want to reverse the physics of stars and hear soft snow unravel its nightgown in the street of another country.

I suppose that's why I can send out work like I was paying a bill: it goes out/it comes back, and over time, more *little* rewards! Publishing's each *petit mort* having its accumulative effect: the pleasure and wisdom of age. Sure, I will be stumbling behind time, but not without a fight. Ever ignited by this irregular art, I want to lucid dream the *"form on the pillow humming while"* I sleep. So, now that I am 60 with sixty heartbeats per minute, looking over one beautiful green precipice of then-was-now, I can say, without *jumping the gun*, that I am like Emile Zola, still living out loud and dying happy while doing it!

Ah! douce campagna, honey in the heart . . .

AND THIS IS ALL I HAVE TO SHOW FOR IT

PATRICK BIZZARO

We turn to last poems at whatever age because we both desire and fear finalities.

—Harold Bloom, *Till I End My Song*

In age one is oneself reflective, both of what it has been to live and of what that act has become as a resonance . . . in memory—what it all meant, so to speak, what it had felt like.

—Robert Creeley, "Reflections on Whitman in Age"

NEARLY TWENTY YEARS AGO, in reviewing a collection of posthumously published poems—*The Guests at the Gate* by my friend and former teacher Anthony Piccione—I acknowledged my profound interest in eschatology as represented in "final poems"[1] by poets of my generation whom I have known and learned from. Having little frame of reference, then, for the task ahead of me, I created artificial boundaries to funnel my observations. Here is how I articulated those boundaries that enabled me at the time to clarify what I meant by the term *final poems*:

---

[1] Harold Bloom, in *Till I End My Song* posits three categories of "last poems": final poems, poems that mark the end, and poems that reflect an imaginative conclusion to a poetic career. In this essay, by "final poems" I mean those published late in a poet's life, or supposedly so, due to their appearance in a collection of posthumously published poems. Thus, my interest is closer to Bloom's "last poems" than to either of his other two categories.

On one side, I would imagine (as I suspect many readers might) Dylan Thomas's "Do Not Go Gentle into That Good Night." One extreme in a poet's advice concerning final events may very well be Thomas's famous, "Rage, rage against the dying of the light." The other extreme would have to be advice more comforting, more accepting, less hopelessly Promethean. Though writing about a different kind of finality, in "Valediction: Forbidding Mourning," John Donne offers a different view entirely, urging us to depart as silently as breath leaving the body. (Donne writes: "So let us melt, and make no noise") ("Awake and marveling," 55)

This effort seems all these years later to have been a worthy start, even if an incomplete one, that I am trying to complete here, and I think I still agree that our final poems tend to look back at relationships as well as forward to eternity and whatever that might hold. I mean, what other choices do we have? But literary history is filled with poems by poets concerned with how they will be understood by readers of the future. It seems poets like to reconcile differences with people from their pasts and also ponder the unknown. Sometimes these tasks get done in the same poem. But I'd want to add to that early contemplation of final poems that each poet will have a different take on how to say goodbye. So it seems worth the effort to look briefly at poems by authors who pushed the limits of that genre we have come to call "last poems" (or established those limits) in their efforts to make a last message concerning how poets perceive the opportunity and license that comes with writing a final poem. There is nothing definitive here, and I don't pretend to have gotten it right in this short essay. Rather, I want to write with the humility my friend Piccione wrote with when he said in one of his last poems, "This is only my way."

Piccione was a prototype contemporary Transcendentalist who wrote in the tradition of a Whitman or an Emerson:

I keep staggering about, wrong name, wrong face,
I'd like to stay for once inside a town,
to fix cars or want to, or work for the railroad,
deliver the mail, consult seriously with others.

I want to come in, start over, forget altogether
that the star giver breathes in us, that we stumble on.
("In Cool Twilight")

I had long admired my friend's empathy in connecting with people, his willingness "to come in, start over, forget altogether." I remember our conversations about Whitman on Tony's farm outside Brockport, NY. How nice it must have been for Tony to be able to articulate these particular thoughts. I continue to shake my head in admiration for what he was able to see and feel. And I've concluded that you just can't make yourself that way and that there is no college course that, by itself, enlarges your soul.

Piccione has another poem in that volume that brings me around to how limited my "youthful" view of final causes was at the time I tried to articulate it. It's as if I had just then thought about something quite distant in the future. Here's Piccione's version of epiphany in "Going Outside as Though I Suddenly Thought of Something." This poem, with the poet "down on the grass," reinforces for me his connection to Whitman. What a wonderful life, to love it "nearly too long to remember!"

Nearing home, I grow very tired and lie down on the grass.
How delicious, to love a life nearly too long to remember!
This is only my way, I am guessing, and walk on into myself.

Piccione is teaching me again as I write this essay that it might be true that all any poet can do is portray a way of thinking about their last days on the planet in a manner that is "only" their way. If this notion is true, then any framework I might have thought was relevant twenty years ago could only be tentative in the face of many final poems that have been written. Maybe what we have are poems about what we know or have known and what we will find out when we enter the eternal. But there is also the issue of legacy to consider, I think.

Over the years you just encounter such final poems matter-of-factly, and they don't make the impact they will once you cross 60 years of age, a kind of finish line for many people who are no longer writing only for tenure or promotion or merit pay. Writing becomes something quite different, maybe more purposeful. Two poems that I think deserve some attention here because they seem purposeful to me are "Someone of the past" by David Ignatow and Denise Levertov's "Immersion" from her posthumous collection *This Great Unknown*. I am drawn to these two poets quite personally because I felt their influence in my life as a young student who was just beginning to write poetry. I met Ignatow at a conference where I read from my first book, *Ohio Seduction*, which Ignatow's poems greatly influenced, at the University of Hartford in the late 1970s, and Levertov a decade before that after a reading she gave, introduced to her as "the football player who was majoring in English." How odd to remember! The poems they left behind interest me not only because I met the poets and studied their works and very different styles, but also because they seem to be looking in different directions. Ignatow's sorrow and maybe regret is over a past relationship in which he seems to have done some harm and now wants forgiveness. Levertov takes a look at the bigger issue of entering eternity uncertain of what to expect there "because of God's silence."

Ignatow's beautiful poem begins with the sense that death is an ongoing metaphor through which we reach some calm reconciliation late in our lives. I love Ignatow's restraint in these lines:

> Someone of the past is dying in front of me,
> Her face immobile,
> She sees herself in me, dying too.

In a style characteristic of many of his poems, Ignatow keeps the poem's intentions unclear so that we are not sure if the issue is physical death or the end of a relationship. I have seen myself die in other people's eyes, even seen myself dead there. Sad but true, most of us have. We seem to become prepared for the death of our physical being by practicing certain kinds of deaths while still wearing our bodies. Ignatow keeps "Someone of the past" open to multiple interpretations until the last stanza offers a surprise moral, a tactic that characterizes an Ignatow poem, and we come to see that this break up is not an impersonal one. It is more private than impersonal, if there's a distinction there: "What we know of each other is dying with us,/ no one else will ever know." The poet longs to relive moments so that harm done in the past will be forgiven. There is powerful regret in these lines, unlike the defiance of the Thomas poem or the acquiescence of the Donne. Ignatow broadens my artificial framework for understanding final poems:

> Did I mean you harm
> When we lived together?
> Did you mean me to be a nightmare
> In your life?

The death Ignatow writes about parallels the death Donne remarks on. But the notion that the poet remembers himself as "a nightmare" in her life complicates with something more dramatic the whole notion of breaking up as a kind of death.

Levertov writes a different kind of last poem by taking on a larger and more universally applicable issue in "Immersion." She reflects more generally on final events than Ignatow does in "Someone of the past." The question of one's relationship with God is ongoing for most, as it was for Levertov. For me the question is whether, in the end, we should trust in science or believe in the often contradictory dogmas of religion, as I will show below. For Levertov in this poem the issue is God's seemingly impersonal immersion in our lives through "events of grace" and "horrifying scrolls of history." The poem contrasts "our own words" with "the holy voice." God's immersion in us is through *our* articulation in *our* language of *His* existence. It is through the concept of eternity that we find "a way to ask" about death and the afterlife, but also a way in Levertov's view in this poem to find the answer to our questions. Without an answer, "There is anger abroad in the world, a numb thunder." But expecting God to tell us what to believe about the afterlife is "naïve," in Levertov's words, because God has already given us words to express our beliefs. At least on the surface, this situation seems to me a more complicated one than regret over a break up earlier in our lives. But I also find myself in my most recent poems, all written since I turned 70, wanting to ask the big questions and trying really hard to not take back behavior of my youth. I'd like to end without regret. To quote Piccione, "This is only my way, I am guessing."

Levertov takes what I think of as the "big view" of mortality. We are not the sum total of our life behaviors. We live, according to the Levertov poem, in order to see the acts through which God speaks to us, acts of grace but also horrifying historical events, in which God is "surely" a calming and reassuring presence not just for now but for all eternity, however long that may be. But as my late father-in-law might say, in a far less philosophic vein, "God give you a brain." It is up to us to see God's presence in the world as a force that, in Levertov's beautiful expression, is "trying to immerse us in a different language" and "in myriad musics, in signs and portents."

Forgive my self-indulgence here. I chose authors who profoundly influenced my thinking but also my path through the life that I've lived so far as a poet. How fundamental to our way of seeing final poems that one took me to her thinking about the eternal and the other to the rectifying past events of his temporal life. Maybe the poems here demonstrate a completely different range of final poems than I could conceive of twenty years ago. In any case, in 2020 I use these two to aid my understanding as I find my way through the poetry I have written during what must surely be my last years.

I appreciate the opportunity to reflect on these important voices that seem a constant inspiration in my life at this juncture of my lifetime. Lucky enough, then, to qualify by age and interest for this collection of essays, I hope to salvage from my recently completed book of poems, *Dictation Dilemma*, four poems that I think justify my thinking as an aged (read "mature") writer facing eternity. I remind you of Piccione's statement that "This is only my way."

One poem I wrote for the much beloved and greatly missed poet and pedagogue Wendy Bishop. I think it's not about building a house necessarily but, rather, concerned with other people building a house made by using what we've left behind, our legacies.

Houses of History
for Wendy Bishop

In the lot
across the street, four men enter
my vision, all doing almost
what I think they're doing,

all building a house,
cooperating in the movement of dirt
to a designated spot across the yard,
all building one house
from a single plan.

But as I watch, I see
ahead of their weary motions
the house of my understanding
and the house of theirs
though all the while
they ignore me

as if the structures we live by
differ at the brick foundation,
and the house this will become
is finished as they begin it,
stretched to its imaginary posts,
so people we have never seen
can enter and make it
a house of their own.

I am just one of many whose life and vocation were influenced by
Wendy. The poem says mostly what I want it to say about what I think
happens to our intellectual property when we march on. Like Pluto, as I
say in another poem in that collection, for another recently departed friend,
Mike Hamer, we become "just a sightless eye / turned away from our galaxy."

Lucky enough late in my life to become husband to Indigenous Studies
scholar Resa Crane and late-life father to our child, Antonio Bizzaro, some
of the failings of my memory are profoundly apparent to me.

At School They Learn Their Nouns
for Antonio

My son's teacher says,
"the children are learning their nouns."

What fun that they should be
learning theirs as I am
forgetting mine.

Where do they go,
these words that name
people, places, and things?
I imagine them spiraling off
like star dust
into the universe,
to become solar systems
of their own,
hanging there
in the galaxy of my life,
until inevitably
a black hole sucks them
out of my memory
leaving them alone,
nameless and forgotten.

Loss of memory—especially recollection of names—precedes the physical demise of many of us. And the question, "Where do they go?" echoes my concern in my poem for Wendy and is intended as serious, which forces many of us to reconcile our understandings of science with our religious beliefs. For me, this juxtapositioning of religion and science has, to a large extent, driven my late life poetry as it allows me to delve into questions of final causes.

The poem becomes more specific and more personal as I recall the central theme of my science classes that "gravity holds us to our chairs / in our classrooms on earth / under the aspect of eternity." But the late-life me also recalls drawings on church walls of my youth that defy gravity, as religion often does:

But religion is different, isn't it?
In the holy image of our deaths,
portraits of the dead show
how the spirit flies
—upwards, outwards—
into the universe in chaos.

We are driven in old age to reach some sort of conclusion based on the evidence accumulated during our lifetimes:

> To fly after death is to break free of earthly science
> and into prayer we imagine
> will free us of laws
> to enter the universe
> as it was meant to be, free
> of restriction.

So the title of this poem is in some ways earned: "Science Under the Aspect of Eternity Is Religion." And I hope my dearly departed, friend-collaborator Mike Hamer knows that he has continued to get me to think about who and what we are.

> Under the aspect of existence
> our lives are no longer governed
> by science and its methods
> that begin and end in faith.

We write to mark the passing of loved ones (too many to include here) and to let those who we expect will outlive us know we have loved them even as we prepare to leave the estate, wishing for a second chance.

LEAVING THE ESTATE
for Jason, my son

> Eviction always comes
> when you need new shoes.
> You're in no mood
>
> for a walk. You're in no
> particular mood at all.
> But you're better off
>
> walking than watching
> slim-hipped hunger
> lick your bowl of dust.

You're better off giving
the abandoned children next door
the lonely space beneath

your winter blanket.
Evicted and lost, you get
what everyone wants—

a second chance—
like the gray-haired man
who withdraws

his savings
from the meager estate
of his youth.

WORKS CITED

Bizzaro, Patrick. "Awake and Marveling." *Tar River Poetry* 42.1 (fall 2002): 55-57.

———. *Ohio Seduction.* West Hartford: Bartholomew's Cobble Press, 1976.

Bloom, Harold. *Till I End My Song: A Gathering of Last Poems.* NY: Harper, 2010.

Creeley, Robert. *On Earth: Last Poems and An Essay.* Berkeley: University of California Press, 2006.

Ignatow, David. "Someone of the Past." *Living is What I Wanted: Last Poems.* Rochester, NY: BOA Editions, Ltd., 1999. Page 28.

Levertov, Denise. "Immersion." *The Great Unknown: Last Poems.* NY: New Directions, 2006. Page 42.

Piccione, Anthony. *The Guests at the Gate.* Rochester, NY: BOA Editions, Ltd., 2002. Page 57.

TIME, MEMORY, SILENCE, & THE ANXIETY OF ENDING

MARK IRWIN

JORGE LUIS BORGES'S memorable short story, "The Captive," tells of a boy in Junin who disappears after an Indian attack. His parents search in vain for him, and many years later a soldier tells of an Indian with blue eyes—possibly the missing son. The parents are in fact reunited, and the boy, now wild and having forgotten his former language, stands incomprehensible before the door of his former house, then rushes in, runs toward the chimney and reaches his hand up, retrieving a "horn-handled knife" that he had hidden many years ago. Here the narrative says, "His eyes shone with joy and the parents wept because they had found their son,"[1] but the boy, disrupted, soon leaves to rejoin his wilderness. Toward the story's end, the narrator asks in a great sense of disjunction, "I wonder what he felt in that dizzying moment when past and present became one."[2]

We are all captives of time, and within time we are captives of memory and habit. For the boy from Junin, the wild habitat had become the new habit that replaced the old, while the keen memory of a knife—in retrospect—seems a transit to the wilderness, the threshold of disappearance.

---

[1] Borges, Jorge Luis. *Collected Fictions.* Anthony Hurley, trans. (New York: Penguin Books, 1999), p. 300.

[2] Ibid., 300.

Yet, the language of this knife in memory will become much more fluent in that wilderness. The knife's relation to reality is renewed.

Becoming older, I am more obsessed with the way that important writers carve out notions of mortality through space and time, and also with something Caravaggio said—"in art there is nothing more difficult than simplicity." Think of Matisse's final drawings of the human figure often composed of one sinuous, transporting line—almost a bridge to another world. Thus, too, in poetry. Here is my translation of Jean Follain's memorable "Vie."

Life

A child is born
into a great landscape
half a century later
he's just a dead soldier
and this was the man
we saw appear and set down
a heavy sack of apples
two or three of which rolled
making sound among sounds of a world
where the bird sang on the door's
stone threshold.[3]

Here, not only does time collapse within four lines (child to dead soldier), but time is marvelously dilated as "two or three" apples roll from a sack. One can hear this most effectively in line nine through the anaphora and monosyllabic words that I use in attempt to protract the event: "making sound among sounds of a world" (bruit parmi ceux d'un monde). The poem ends with the bird singing not only in this same "world," but from a threshold, singing almost through the dilated sound of those apples. After practicing law for several decades, Follain finally retired as a judge in Charleville, and though he lived a life immersed in poetry and painting, his poem almost reads in a legal sense as a *brief* of a brief—one of life.

---

[3] Follain, Jean. *Transparence du monde.* (Paris: Gallimard,1943), p.27.

The manner by which poets shape space and time becomes much more complex and architectural as they age. Consider the wide-ranging use of space in Arthur Sze's "Sight Lines," the title poem of his tenth collection published in 2019. A master of shifting perspective and perception, Sze employs geographical, scientific, historical, governmental, physical, and spiritual "sight lines" as he writes a treatise on contemporary America guised in a love poem. Here are lines three to six:

> the snowpack in the Sangre de Christos has already dwindled before
>   spring—
> at least no fires erupt in the conifers above Los Alamos—
> the plutonium waste has been hauled to an underground site—
> a man who built plutonium triggers breeds horses now—
> no one could anticipate this distance from Monticello—[4]

As Sze works the aquifers on his own land outside Santa Fe, these channels radiate from the ontological toward the intimate and disjunctive historical. Jefferson, the architect of *The Declaration of Independence*, evinces no less disjunction (through his use of slavery) than the physicist who "built plutonium triggers" and now breeds horses. Sze's step here is of enormous consequences and passion:

> I step out of the ditch but deeper into myself—
> I arrive at a space that no longer needs autumn or spring . . .
>
> though you are visiting Paris, you are at my fingertips—
> though I step back into the ditch, no whitening cloud dispels this world's
>   mystery—
> the ditch ran before the year of the Louisiana Purchase—
> I'm walking on silt, glimpsing horses in the field—
> fielding the shapes of our bodies in white sand—
> though parallel lines touch in the infinite, the infinite is here—[5]

---

[4] Sze, Arthur. *Sight Lines*. (Port Townsend: Copper Canyon Press, 2019), p. 53.

[5] Ibid., p. 54.

Both the aquifer channels and terrifying, perceptual sight lines continue to radiate outward; the speaker finds calm in the infinite present, or as Emmanuel Levinas says, "The excess over the present is the life of the Infinite."[6]

Before dying, my grandmother Marie, a widow, would often play two TVs at once in the house, two TVs cranked at high volume and she wasn't deaf, but perhaps this was a companion of sorts, and also a way to push away death. Yes, there are two ways to accept death: to push the silence away or to embrace it. I'm much more interested in the latter and how we find it in the mid to late works of writers. Here's the opening of Yeats's "After Long Silence":

> Speech after long silence; it is right,
> All other lovers being estranged or dead,
> Unfriendly lamplight hid under its shade,
> The curtains drawn upon unfriendly night,[7]

—And so it is with writing after long silence—moving deeply there, embracing it. I love Marguerite Duras's definition of what it means "to write." Here's my translation from *Écrire*:

> To write is also to not speak.
> It is to be silent.
> It is to howl without any sound.[8]

Listen to how this works in Robert Creeley's small, but magnificent "Echo" from *Memory Gardens*.

> Back in time
> for supper
> when the lights[9]

---

[6] Levinas, Emmanuel. *Otherwise Than Being*, trans. Alphonso Lingis (Pittsburgh: Duquesne UP, 2006), p. 195.

[7] Yeats, W.B. *Selected Poems and Plays*. M.L. Rosenthal, ed. (New York: Macmillan, 1962), p. 147.

[8] Duras, Marguerite. *Ecrire*. (Paris: Gallimard, 1993), 31.

[9] Creeley, Robert. *Just in Time: Poems (1984–1994)*. (New York: New Directions, 2001), p. 39.

The poem, unpunctuated, plumbs silence through memory and light, a silence heightened by that *rushing* in childhood, that hurrying back from play. Its abstract power is achieved through the title, "Echo," which finds disjunctive equivalents through sound and light. Light *echoes* so to speak, sped up by the enjambed syntax. Consciousness becomes a loop through memory triggered by light, that light in memory triggered once again by the present light as it occurs in the poem. Its syllabics begin to provide a clue: three tri-syllabic lines that scan as

/ u /
u / u
/ u /.

The final monosyllabic stress on "lights" allows the poem to shine its way, to return to its beginning, such that the effect is a flickering in eternity, a symphonic loop of sorts where the first and last chords are similarly stressed. The word "supper," the only non-monosyllabic word, is heartbreaking, for it is always a last, yet lasting supper in memory, and because the poem has nine words, the haunting center falls somewhere between "for" and "sup," a forever sip that can never be still completely, but one illumined again and again, lit with the eternity of a Vermeer painting.

I've written a great deal about time, space, and silence thus far, something introduced by the Borges story in which the boy from Junin, briefly reunited with his parents, flees to the wilderness after retrieving a knife he had hidden. As a poet, I've always felt close to two types of wilderness—the natural world and language—and in both I seek silence among the populated sounds. Silence, where time and space become one as in a canvas painted all white. When a former partner died, I kept painting my studio white—coat after coat as though I were listening—close. I kept painting white over shadow, painting white over any noise until I could write again. This is what I wrote:

> Now light turns the room a deep orange at dusk and you
> think you are floating, but in truth you are falling, and the fall
> is so slow, yet precise, like climbing a ladder of straw. Now
> leaning forward, you open your hands that keep opening. Is
> this what *Yes* feels like? Making a shore where no water was? [10]

---

[10] Irwin, Mark. *Shimmer*. (Tallahassee: Anhinga Press, 2020), p.11.

I'm a great fan of Emily Dickinson's insoluble disproportion of time and space, and how in the fourth stanza of "I Felt a Funeral in My Brain," she carves an enormous silence:

> As all the Heavens were a Bell,
> And Being, but an Ear,
> And I, and Silence, some strange Race
> Wrecked, solitary, here— [11]

The nearness to death here is keenly imagistic and philosophical. Although bell and ear share inverse shapes in their similarity, the vastness of this Heaven's "Bell" might only transmit upon death to Being's "Ear."—And to what would it listen, and how in the gleaning silence? —A silence that engenders a kind of foot "Race," spirit "Race," or new "Race" of people? —A silence whose unique wreckage will be total and solitary.

Consider the silence in Donald Revell's poem "Rapture," whose disjunctive title rises above the body of text that mixes the tainted lives of humans with the lives of sparrows, whose gregarious and continual singing-nature becomes a symbol of both spirit and self-worth. A domestic and common bird, here its "cape of shadow" thrown by flocks becomes the "shape of men," perhaps in an area of spirit unattainable for humans. The poem's haunting silence is achieved through the assonance of "o" sounds that gradually pool in the word "no." Here are the first two stanzas:

> Sparrow is footfalls
> Cape of shadows
> Shape of men
> Where no men
> Ought to be
>
> Song comes after
> Briefly if ever
> In blind air [12]

---

[11] Dickinson, Emily. *Complete Poems of Emily Dickinson*, ed. Thomas Johnson (Boston: Little, Brown, 1960), p. 42.

[12] Revell, Donald. *Tantivy*. (Farmington, Maine: Alice James Books, 2012), p. 39.

Revell's poem menaces patriarchal vision ("Where no men / Ought to be") and is subtle, abstract, yet convinced by its high music where the avian life of spirit shadows that of humans and morality.

> I have seen
> A sparrow becoming
> The world's end [13]

As I continue to age, I often feel an anxiety when ending a poem, something experienced near the final stanzas, though I have no idea what those lines might be—an anxiety that might involve taking a walk, doing something in the garden, or listening to a favorite passage of music—anything that might provide a more language-present, layered, or surprising *removal of intent*. It is a "great responsibility" to end a poem, just as it is to think of people no longer here, something that I articulate in the first poem from my tenth collection entitled *Shimmer*:

> What a great responsibility to speak of people no longer here.

> What a great responsibility to know that each *I* on the page leans
>   toward the horizon
> while the living lie down with the dead.[14]

—*Los Angeles, October 2020*

---

[13] Ibid., p. 39.

[14] Irwin, p. 3.

DEATH IS THE MOTHER OF BEAUTY

CATHRYN COLMAN

ON SOME LEVEL, we write/create because we know, consciously or not, that we will die. As I write, my interest in the liminal holds a powerful space for beauty. As a musician I learned that the silence between each note, between each chord, or movement, is just as important as the written score. When I play the piano, an ineffable conversation occurs between my fingers, the keys, and the music. This liminal, this "in-between" place feels generative and mysterious, where surprise and the unconscious abide. I never know what I'm going to write about before I write. I use a list of random words and phrases to get going. Loss, death and time are major subjects for me. A young student of mine said, "When you're young, you write about love. When you're old, you write about death." But I still write about love and its many whole and beautifully broken forms.

My recent book, *Time Crunch*, contains a series of elegiac poems about my favorite writers, painters, actors, and musicians, sometimes adopting personas to imitate their voices and predilections—sometimes using lineation to evoke the artist's style. For early collage artist, Kurt Schwitters, I collaged the poem. For jazz pianist and composer, Thelonius Monk, I mimicked his quirky, on-the-spectrum genius rhythms, his lyricism, and his dissonance. Hoping that beauty follows, I write towards an indefinable place of truth where my late mother was Muse, much like Marcel Proust's mother was for him. When I finished a poem, my mother was the first one to hear it and talk to me about it.

I like my ideas "on ice." I write better when it's cold, always heading north for writing retreats. True north is where one might find a writer's last words. Jane Austen's last words were: "I want nothing but death." James Joyce: "Doesn't anyone understand?" Thoreau's inscrutable "Moose . . . Indian" and Hemingway's "Goodnight, Kitten" to his wife, right before he killed himself. Oscar Wilde: "This wallpaper and I are fighting a duel to the death. Either it goes or I do." And Alfred Jarry, the French Dada/Surrealist writer who died asking for a toothpick. I know my last words will be waiting for me, patient as a mother with her sick child.

When I think back on my life, it comes to me in scenes as if from a film. As a student at University of California, Berkeley, my boyfriend and I get tear-gassed by the National Guard while protesting the war in Vietnam. We, with hundreds of others, eventually shut down the school. That summer, sans eye irritants, Richard Misrach, the photographer, and I go camping for three months up the coast and across Canada. We get so stoned on the Olympic Peninsula eating just-caught salmon at the beach with strangers, that we can't find the trail back up to the VW van and have to sleep in the dirt. Thanksgiving at my parent's house in Los Angeles includes actors, such as Tony Randall, Doris Day, Ginger Rogers and Walter Matthau. Tony Randall keeps correcting my English. "You say 'like' too much!" he admonishes. This whole gathering reminds me of a slightly weird dream. Susanne Langer, brilliant philosopher and writer about aesthetics, said that every art form has a primary illusion. The primary illusion of music is passing time. The primary illusion of the novel is memory. The primary illusion of film is dream. So jump cut to the 1980's, where I watch TV news late at night in a canyon cottage and am shocked to see my father get out of a limousine with Elizabeth Taylor on his tuxedoed arm. I try to live in Manhattan, where I was born, and I'm so broke I only have two pairs of shoes and eat dinner at happy hours across the city, assessing which ones have the best spread.

When I work as an assistant for Martin Scorsese (in his films the phantom was *always* at the feast), we all live in his rented house in LA: his chef, Dan, who had been a mercenary in Angola, Robbie Robertson, Isabella Rossellini, and his bodyguard, Steven Prince. After *Taxi Driver* someone had made an attempt on Scorsese's life. Steven always came down to breakfast with a gun in his underwear band. He had quite an extensive arsenal and told such vivid stories they inspired Marty to make a documentary film about him called *An American Boy*. Years later, to concentrate on our work, novelist Tracy DeBrincat and I rent W.S. Merwin's three hundred-year-old farmhouse in the Dordogne, France. One of the rules is that we must not kill *anything*. It is 2 a.m. in the kitchen when I confront a black-haired, meaty spider, big as my hand. Together we make the shortest horror film in history. After a few minutes, it scuttles back under the antique armoire.

In graduate school, I almost lose my mind studying for my orals by making a chart of the universe to connect the works of Virginia Woolf, Gerard Manley Hopkins and Theodore Roethke. But no matter what is happening, even when I have three jobs and am working my way through school, or I have two jobs and work by day as a receptionist for a mean comedian in a skyscraper who has prostitutes up to the office, I always manage to eke out some writing. Because when you really love something and long to learn, you sit at the feet of the master. My mentor was the late, great, poet Stan Rice, who taught me Wallace Stevens, H.D., Ginsberg, Sappho, etc. Stan opened the world of poetry to me in a way that became addictive. He was the Mick Jagger of modern poetry. People left his lectures high, as if they had just been to an amazing rock concert. I credit him for planting the seed that grew slowly but steadily over the years.

I was always a voracious reader. Growing up, my brother told me I was either out with friends or in my room reading. This was also an act of survival: to absent myself from the emotionally violent relationship between my parents. All that reading affected my writing, my love of words, my vocabulary. I traveled extensively. But nothing can prepare one for loss: close and best friends dying young, from cancer and AIDS, my mother dying one day without ever being sick, the feeling of a strong, healthy body I no longer have due to a pain condition. But so far, I still have words to mediate these losses. To investigate them. To pour my sorrow into one vessel. I have words and I have moments. I still have that thrilling, coloratura high C, Rilke's Duino Elegies, and that feeling when you get the poem just right and it shines. Or as Stan would say, "It crackles hard." Continually obsessed by death throughout my life, I drive across the Bay Bridge at night to school and my hands want to turn the wheel into the white wall, just like Christopher Walken in *Annie Hall*. I take speed, cocaine, Quaaludes, brandy, and pot at the same time. I take Black Beauties and mescaline. I have sex with handsome, random strangers, once in a restaurant bathroom. We didn't order anything. This isn't about death exactly, but it is about danger/adjacent altered states. I hike five hours a day over many mountains and, one summer, I hike way up to a ghost town in Aspen. Like an approaching train, a big storm billows and explodes over me. The shivering trees and huge thunder-shadows crack open the sky, its light dipping all the leaves in silver foil. The world looks remade, strangely gorgeous, yet I become sick, almost paralyzed with intense anxiety. Later, I discover that I had experienced Stendhal's Syndrome: a psychosomatic condition that can involve rapid heartbeat, fainting, even hallucinations when one experiences phenomena of great beauty. Stendhal experienced this in Florence, Italy, hence the moniker. Miles away from humans, I am wet to the skin in downpour, disoriented, and completely ecstatic.

This essay's title comes from Wallace Stevens' poem "Harmonium" (1923). Death and it's ally Time, are leitmotifs beneath all our poetry, all our art. So many memento mori paintings (from the Renaissance and onward) include skulls or dying flowers nearly hidden by live objects. Early Christians greeted each other with the words "Remember your death." Nuns had human skulls on their desks. From Edgar Degas's surprising painting of a skull smoking a cigarette to Gerhard Richter's magnificent *Skull* that mourns the loss of humanity—skulls are numerous and ubiquitous across art forms since early cave paintings, reminding us that death in life must not be forgotten. That we are finite beings.

As I age towards my seventh decade, I realize I still suffer from "never enough" or "not good enough." Our poems are never good enough. We haven't written enough books. We're not recognized enough. I remember standing over Keats's tombstone in Rome, Italy that says "Here lies one whose name is writ in water." Well, pour a bucket of it over my head. Or give me the ice cube challenge. Move over, John. This, plus some childhood trauma, always lead to more "I'm not enough." Is it because I'm Jewish and we have that internalized denigration in our genes? Who knows? Virginia Woolf talked about death as the one experience she would not be able to write about. Her (in my opinion) greatest book, *The Waves,* ends with a rant against death, triumphing over death. But that was fiction. I stand in her backyard under her oak tree by the River Ouse where she drowned herself and think, I want to pick up a rock and sneak it into my baggage. So I do.

There is no way to stop the arrow of time. It flies with us. That's why the last stanza of W.C. William's poem "The Sparrow" always moves me. "This was I, a sparrow. / I did my best; farewell." It's okay to just be. Relax. Stop beating yourself. Against the tenet of many Angelenos, whom I call Positive Thinking Nazis, I quote Wittgenstein, "I don't know why we're here, but I'm pretty sure it's not to enjoy ourselves." This is not to say that I don't have moments of joy and connection. But when I realize I've been aware of the planet's danger and extinction since global warming was called "the greenhouse effect," I worry that we're also losing sacred totems of inspiration, of salvation. We're losing language. When I see the changing global politics, the atrocities, the seditious attacks, the move towards Fascism with its concurrent racism, sexism and anti-Semitism, I feel disheartened. At the moment, the rise in marches and demonstrations gives me hope. The powerful, vital Black Lives Matter movement and the protests against gun violence certainly have death and life in them. And how fucking difficult is it to wear a mask?

Even if I can't or don't write another word, I know for awhile longer, I will have nature and my relationship with the being-ness of trees. When I'm in a forest, silent poems form deep inside my brain. The forest not only makes paper, but it also writes on paper through me.

> "Live in the layers,
>   not in the litter.
> Though I lack the art
>   to decipher it,
> no doubt the next chapter
> in my book of transformations
> is already written.
> I'm not done with my changes."
>   —Stanley Kunitz, from "The Layers"

WHAT POETS KNOW: DRY AND WET (GENERATIONAL AUTHORITY IN THE ARTS)

RICHARD KATROVAS

Humankind cannot bear very much reality.

—T.S. Eliot, *The Four Quartets*

I AWOKE THIS past Tuesday astonished that I am 66. I'd been 66 on the previous Monday, too, but had not been astonished. Indeed, I had been, last Monday, 66 for almost a 150 days, but had not been astonished until I awoke that otherwise innocuous early spring day, a Tuesday, and realized, even as I drew my first conscious breath, that I am no longer middle-aged, that I am light years from my youth and consequently don't have very long to live. As sudden realizations go, that was a humdinger.

But how could I not have known before last Tuesday that I am old? This question is located in that blurry epistemological space in which there are two kinds of knowing, dry and wet. Dry knowing is the apprehension of information that has not been dragged through the blood-soaked rag and bone shop of the heart; wet knowing is drenched in the fear of extinction. In a state of dry knowing, I'd dovetailed my personal mortality with mortality generally. This past Tuesday at 6:28 a.m., my death came a-knockin' on my dream-soaked noggin!

I know that the Holocaust happened, and that it was a singularly horrendous event. How can anyone know, in the same sense that Thomas is reported to have known, that a world-historical event is not simply a fictional narrative, which is to say a lie (a young dead guy named Jesus reanimates, encounters one of his homeys who, astonished, actually diddles a fresh, deep wound in the charismatic fellow's lower torso) or a myth (a lie that nonetheless reflects a tragic truth of consciousness, that we require the impossible)? As inexplicable as I regard Holocaust denial to be, the fact that my knowing is (usually) dry blunts empathy by virtue of the fact that my imagination has not been deployed, has not been goose-stepped to active duty, has not herded the horror toward a representative micro-event, that is, to something that a person can wrap her or his proverbial head around. Dry knowing often centers on the apprehension of macro-horror, an essential objectifying of horrendous events such that they may be processed, which is to say imagined in broad outline, which is also to say not imagined at all except in that dispassionate way that the benign shenanigans of cosmology are conceived beyond both numbers and images, that is, abstractly in a *nonmathematical* sense, though perhaps in a mathematical sense, too, if we understand the exact number of atoms in the sun, at any given nanosecond, to be as meaningless as the number of angels that can dance on the head of a pin, or, more to the point, as meaningless as the Biblical designation of forty days and forty nights, or the rounded figure of six million when designating the number of murders over the course of the Shoah. By "meaningless" I mean, in the truest sense, unfathomable. Dry knowing occurs without emotional investment, or at least without the pretense, or fact, of emotional connection.

"Reality," or truth's relation to reality, is a function of wet knowing, of verifiable data that is simultaneously apprehended and felt. Needless to say, neither you nor I can deploy empathy in sufficient measure to encompass world-historical machinations and their brutal consequences.

And yet History squats on our chests as we lie awake in the dark, grows heavier and, over time, oddly, more bearable. Existential dread is born of the mere possibility that life, as such, is *nothing but* a "disease of matter," as both Goethe and Mann are credited with first noting. Yet "nothing but" is my Am'r'can rhetorical imposition upon Teutonic perspicacity; no one who truly believes that life is nothing but a disease of matter would even bother getting out of bed to do anything but jump out a high window or chug a Drano-Clorox cocktail. Stipulating that all life is a disease of matter, one posits that its origin is meaningless, not that it is meaningless as such, and "nothing but" is only the unpersuasively punkish swagger with which one may whistle past the contagion ward on one's stroll to the cemetery. Existential dread is nothing but "nothing but," a knee-jerk howl at the new moon of our ravenous need to fill the universe with our singularity, to subsume It All.

Lest I drift on the Jet Stream of my fancy into a neo-hippie stupor, I'll stipulate that life is a disease of matter, *but* that it is not just that. It is as meaningful as the biological imperative to survive, and as the urge to self-expression beyond creature needs but *in relation to those needs in* similar fashion as is posited between two quantum entities displaying Spooky Action at a Distance.

My biological imperative to survive is my link to all that lives, from the shyest amoeba to the most lugubrious pachyderm (or vice versa); my link to my fellow humans is the urge to self-expression, which is a manifestation of the fact that, as Ernest Becker pronounced in his wise and beautiful *The Denial of Death* (Free Press, 1973), we are "angels with anuses." That is, we are biological entities, but we are also symbol-consuming and symbol-making creatures each fully aware that s/he arrives among the living stamped with an indeterminant yet circumscribed shelf date but is also imbued with an irrational desire not only to live forever but to do so while filling the entire universe as a singular awareness. I submit that how we manage that fundamental paradox of human consciousness is the essence of what we call wisdom, and that this wisdom is the essence of art.

I proceed on the quaint belief that there are three kinds of wisdom corresponding to the three stages of life. There is a wisdom of youth, a wisdom of midlife, and a wisdom of old age, and each is discrete. The first does not necessarily segue into the second as one transitions, the second into the third; additionally, the potency of the first diminishes whether one transitions into the second or not, and the potency of the second diminishes whether one segues into the third or not. Indeed, the foolishness of one's youth may be shed as s/he transitions into a wiser midlife, and the foolishness of midlife may evaporate as one assumes the wisdom endemic to decrepitude.

My generation—at the lower end on the verge, and on the higher end in the midst of geriatric bliss—is defined in infantile terms, and coincidentally was the first generation to define itself primarily in opposition to the previous generation's parental authority. At the heart of the sixties/seventies counterculture ethos is a radical egalitarianism that sprayed plumes of Any-Boy-and-Girl-Can-

Make-Art in similar fashion to the DDT trucks' spraying of neighborhood streets in the fifties, many of us galumphing ecstatically behind those toxic beasts as our loving parents looked on in ignorant approval. The Never Land of creative writing shimmers in the mist several miles offshore and down the road, into the highlands, from Brigadoon. Transit from the former to the latter is from treacherous innocence to idyllic indeterminacy. Implicit in pedagogy is generational authority, subset of parental authority, and the *Wanderung* from Never Land to Brigadoon is subcontracted to the Pied Piper of Hamelin, the first tenured poet.

The arc of my career would be the arc of my self-esteem, my sense of social value, if I were deeply traumatized by poor potty training or a too abrupt transition from breastmilk. But I am one Baby Boomer who, I was told when I was too young to appreciate the humor, stood in my crib at ten months and smeared my own feces on a wall, pre-articulating the egocentric predicament in a soporific state of blissful self-expression. For better or worse, I do not require much tribal affirmation, and though I delight in my little career successes, I regard them as incidental to the intrinsic value of what has garnered me those successes, as humble as such efforts have been. The fact is that I feel I am just hitting my proverbial stride at the tender age of 66, that though I found my voice in my 20s, I just didn't know, for the most part, what to do with it. The wisdom of youth, coiled in my loins, struck my frontal lobe a few times, but otherwise relished the dark. Now, I trace the contours of my ignorance as unabashedly as I once traced the contours of the gods' faces on a wall with my shit, and in a state of jubilation no less potent.

According to actuarial tables, the world may stick a fork in me. According to my own hoary heart, I am neither raw nor done; yet I feel a force trying to pull me too soon from the fire, a force that is the collective will of those younger than I wishing for a place not at, but on the banquet table—that they, too, may be joyfully consumed. By what? By whom? Perhaps by ambition, a condition pertaining to career status and tethered to practical lifestyle considerations.

This is no country for old poets, and it isn't amenable to young or midlife poets, either. Poets, literary artists generally (those whose products with rare exception do not sell in airport bookstores), exist in a more or less hermetic loop, as though the exclusive audience for standup comedians were standup comedians. But standup comedy exists in the brutal context of market imperatives, and poetry is wholly subsumed by academe (poetry-slam culture and its auxiliary activities notwithstanding) such that it tends to duplicate academic publication and dissemination; something like peer review replaces, at least augments, market dynamics, though, alas, it is peer review more akin to gang initiation than to academic assessment, and the plethora of high-sounding awards and distinctions that has accrued over the past fifty years or so has everything to do with the incursion of creative writing, particularly poetry, into academe. The Bum Schmuck Award doled out semi-annually by *Your Dirty Drawers Quarterly* could indeed be the clincher for a hiring committee at MLA, and the lucky putz thus welcomed into the Valhalla of Full Employment will seek to garner other such distinctions in pursuit of tenure, a state in which s/he exists as the Po Biz rep at the High Table graced by roasted magic boar flesh and mead that issues from the ut(d)t(d)ers of a magic goat. And thus ensconced, s/he will, consciously or unconsciously, advocate for the general interests of the po biz as those interests seem coterminous with the interests of students who likewise seek admittance to the Hall of Valor, and who relish the battle, the competition, for a vaunted seat at the table (or to grace a silver platter on it).

But unlike the magical groaning board in Valhalla, there are only so many seats at this glorious table, and to the more ambitious, and more socially adept or charismatic regardless of talent or commitment to the art, the table at which they belly up is rounded not exclusively by other warrior poets, but also by scholars of the various categories of literary history, genre, theory, and pedagogy. This is no country for old poets from the POV of young poets seeking steady, protected gigs, places at the table (or on it).

I love my job. I love academe. I love the life that I've been afforded. I don't love poetry any more than I love the earth's molten core, but I love the role of poet, often too much, sometimes not enough. I hate that the Founders of Creative Writing, the (mostly American) poets and writers born anytime from the outbreak of the First World War to the end of the Second, are largely fading from the collective memory of Millennials. I hate that the process of professionalization that the Founders initiated and husbanded has ossified into a cottage industry more dedicated to blind expansion than to cultural enrichment. I despair, just a little, that poets have been tamed, have been admitted, if incrementally and with Kafkaesque caveats, into the polis.

The Baby Boomer poets were mentored by a parent generation for whom the role of poet still afforded exquisite outsider status. The "Greatest Generation" of poets suffered from an enormous shared sense of inferiority relative to their own progenitors, the High Moderns, those who resuscitated, in a manner of speaking, "the dead art of poetry," and in so doing determined, inadvertently, a course toward professionalization.

It is the nature of lyric discourse to shuttle between dry and wet knowing, and to comb, by virtue of its redundant route, from the velvety threads of imagination, the grit of the quotidian. And I am free to make poems and essays about poets and stories and novels and memoirs and any other damned thing I may wish to make, but if I haven't, by this stage of my life, achieved something like a first-tier career status, however that may be judged, will I be allowed, or, to put it more fairly, encouraged, to change, to advance in career status by virtue of present and future creative efforts?

Life expectancy in the US is 78 and seven-tenths years; it's probably higher in my demographic. I bench press over three hundred pounds on a good day. I power walk or jog three miles most days. I do a karate workout intermittently. I'm type-2 diabetic but control the condition with exercise and metformin. I feel consistently better, having quit alcohol several years ago, than I felt for the previous decade or so. All things being equal, I may have at least a good decade of productivity ahead of me.

And my relation to the profession—and yes, my relation to art is one thing, and my relation to the profession quite another—is like that of the persona of Robert Frost's "Two Tramps in Mud Time" to manual labor. The two indigent fellows are thirty or more years younger than I and need the work. But I relish chopping wood in the way that one relishes activity that is not required of him but must get done all the same.

My parent generation of poets, which included Pied Pipers such as Allen Ginsburg and Robert Bly ("tenure" was incidental for both, though both suckled academe for their entire adult lives), conjured careers from the generational breach; to jumble the trope, they were Pied Pipers who led a Children's Crusade, and that holy invasion has settled into a protracted occupation of the unholy but fecund Land of Opportunity, Am'rica, Amerika, Om-erica. They proceeded, at least superficially, from a sense of radical purpose, or radical *repurposing*, to deploy a current popular term, regarding lyric art.

I read Stanley Kunitz's poem "The Layers" when I was in my late 20s, when I was, at least somewhat, on the make for something like a career. I got it—the poem, but the career, too—but in a dry-knowing kind of way. Now, I cannot help but consider it as I am drenched in the exquisite terror issuing from the simple math of my mortality:

The Layers

I have walked through many lives,
some of them my own,
and I am not who I was,
though some principle of being
abides, from which I struggle
not to stray.
When I look behind,
as I am compelled to look
before I can gather strength
to proceed on my journey,
I see the milestones dwindling
toward the horizon
and the slow fires trailing
from the abandoned campsites
over which scavenger angels
wheel on heavy wings.
Oh, I have made myself a tribe
out of my true affections,
and my tribe is scattered!
How shall the heart be reconciled
to its feast of losses?
In a rising wind
the manic dust of my friends,
those who fell along the way,
bitterly stings my face.
Yet I turn, I turn,
exulting somewhat,
with my will intact to go

wherever I need to go,
and every stone on the road
precious to me.
In my darkest night,
when the moon was covered
and I roamed through wreckage,
a nimbus-clouded voice
directed me:
"Live in the layers,
not on the litter."
Though I lack the art
to decipher it,
no doubt the next chapter
in my book of transformations
is already written.
I am not done with my changes.

The professionalization of poetry is not unlike the professionalization of politics, and the consequence is similar: the art part is not diminished just subsumed, though by what? Social ambition that has little (though that bit is important) to do with artistic ambition. The change that I've most recently experienced is from a mild concern for career status to virtually no concern. I am, at the tender age of 66, consumed both by the terror of extinction and the perverse joy of self-expression. But then I can afford, literally, such a shift in perspective, in goals, in fundamental values. I've been tenured for years.

"What Poets Know: Dry and Wet (Generational Authority in the Arts)" appears in Richard Katrovas's forthcoming collection of essays, *Fools Who Love Them: A Memoir in Essays*; Louisiana State University Press.

ARE YOUR AFFAIRS IN ORDER?

GARY SOTO

MY WIFE AND I are into Season 3 of *Victoria*, the Masterpiece Theatre series that seems as long as the queen's monarchial reign. It's a slow-moving narrative in which a teacup is picked up, put down. Then, for dramatic tension, the camera pans to a terrier that, on cue, lifts a hind leg to squirt on the carpet—a barbarous display in the palace household. It's a series that may continue without me, as I may succumb to boredom, the white flag of defeat raised on my chest. My last words: "The DVD is from the library—don't forget to return it."

But in one episode I was stirred awake when Queen Victoria's ex-prime minister—what's his name again?—appears ill in speech and in ash-colored makeup. He won't last long, I understand—the cough, the squeak of violins behind the cough, his fish-pouting mouth, the poor posture in the velvet chair, along with the makeup, of course. A somber doctor stands before the former PM and declares, "Sir, you should put your affairs in order."

That line of advice perked me up. I, ever forward thinking, have a living trust, a document that contains more boilerplate than inventive clauses intended to confuse the taxman. Still, it's done, filed away, and what our daughter will search for when my wife and I are no longer on this planet. We will make it easy for her. We'll leave a trail of Post-its on the hallway wall, which will lead her to my modest office, where a table lamp glows and a faint

Erik Satie sonata plays on my second-hand Bose radio. The final Post-it will say, "The trust is here, darling."

Our money in the bank and the mutual funds—or a third of it at least—will go to nonprofits. But the house and items inside the house—the possessions from forty-three years of marriage—will go to our daughter. She will have to declutter: out with the fourteen pairs of reading glasses, out with the dead batteries, the cotton balls and medicines, the everyday cutlery, the tennis rackets, the potted plants gasping for water on windowsills, the shoes moored like boats in our three closets. The boxed food in the pantry? To the Rescue Mission. The books that stand shoulder to shoulder at the front entrance? Perhaps she will divvy them up to those Little Free Libraries that stand in front of houses in Berkeley—some for you, she might sing, some for you, and you, and you. My attempt at playing filmmaker was short-lived— one half-four production titled *The Pool Party*, on VHS cassette. I have plans for its destruction. I'll run over it many times with my huge American car before I go.

But our art collection is worth pondering for its financial worth. Like housing prices, art has gone skyward. This causes worry. Have I hung them in a way that will cause fading from sunlight? Have they been nibbled by insects with a taste for finer things? I ponder, I muse, and I do sums on my fingers. This DeLoss McGraw, purchased in 2014, what would it fetch? This Rupert Garcia bought in 1984? The Carmen Lomas Garza? The Leo Limon? I'm sure that the works of these artists have gone up in value. A month ago I visited their websites and saw that they are honored and sought after, written about by scholars at universities that don't need street addresses to get their mail.

The artwork, like the Japanese antiques and Mexican folk art, I value for the pleasure it provides. I see them as counterpoints to my poetry. I mean artists and poets should go side by side, right? I'll buy your artwork if you, bearded portraitist with one ear, will drop twenty dollars to purchase a book of mine.

What do I exactly possess? Several pieces by our favorite artist, DeLoss McGraw. From my couch in the living room I can see an irregularly sized pastel on thick paper, 7 inches by 5 feet, titled *Alice in Wonderland*. Alice is blond, fleet of foot, in a red jumper. In spite of the title, there are other figures—and mystical things—of equal metaphorical weight. There's a dove carrying a 3-year-old in a hamper-like black cloth; a boy, also blond, briskly walking; a red rocking horse; and yellow starbursts. The background is bluish, with banner colors of red and yellow, and black-and-white stripes that remind me of piano keys. Purchase price in 2014: $3,000. Today's value? Let's add a couple of zeros, say $30,000, excluding two-day shipping.

Beyond *Alice in Wonderland*, in our tiny, seldom-used dining room are two sepia-colored paintings by McGraw. Each of these untitled and book-sized works beckons to be viewed. One shows a boy upside down, topsy-turvy, mouth open, surprised by his circumstance. He is flanked by a tall building that reminds me of the Leaning Tower of Pisa—plus a chair and a world that appears hoisted up by the powerful winds of a tornado. There is a balloon in the middle that says: "What is after the universe?"

On the other side of the French doors is its twin. While this one is mostly sepia-colored, here we have a spot of color; this boy is also upside down but wears a blue shirt. The top of the building is roofed in blue and what might be a moon—not a splotch—is also blue. The balloon in the middle says: "What was the right answer?"

The twin portraits were bought in 2006 for $425 each. I drum my fingers on my thighs, calculating a new price. In less than a minute, I come up with a figure. Value: $36,000 for the pair. That sounds about right.

Without pushing myself off the couch, I can view more of our art collection. If I swivel my head to the right I look upon two more fanciful McGraws, one of which is an artist proof, number 4. It features a boy, about age 10, dressed in a brown suit with fat, grayish rings around his thighs and knees. On his head a bluish cap, with red stripes, and, as a bill to the cap, what looks like a canary. There are green, blue, red and brown animal-like faces that could be masks; then again, they could be faces of quasi-humans who hanker to make the leap into the animal world. Purchase price in 2004: a gift from the artist! I munch on my lower lip and think. A few seconds and my estimate is tabulated. Value: $47,000. Who could argue?

And to the right of this untitled McGraw is yet another untitled McGraw done with pastels on thick paper. It features a young man who is two-thirds slender legs, a human giraffe if there ever was one. His pants are brown, his shirt red, and his cap of hair a light shade of brown. A few inches from his face he holds a stick with an animal mask—the face of a pony or the face of a bear? He's peering through the mask at a bent-back man who grips a lumpish sack. Behind the man there is a red ladder—McGraw loves ladders. And near the top is a fractured house—McGraw loves houses even more. Purchase price in 2003: another gift from the artist. Without much pondering, my internal auction gavel comes down. Value: $145,000. To wit—poets and artists require three meals a day! And we do require our portion of wines produced in French regions that we'll never visit.

Now I must get up from the couch and take myself down the hallway where hang two other DeLoss McGraw pastels. One features the most adorable couple on the face of the planet: my wife and me in our youth, in our beauty, in the spring of our lives. I am holding a house on fire, presumably lit by the bolt of yellow lightning just above our heads and *presumably* the sensual fire that we would create in our partnership. There are also a red rocking horse, a secondary house, a television on fire, a man-in-the-moon face, a purple and yellow planet, and a whimsy of pinwheels—in short, a Magical Mystery Tour. The work is large—3 feet by 5 feet and, thus, almost life-size if my wife were to stand next to it. Purchase price in 2003: another gift! Current value: $229,000. Unfortunately for art dealers in New York and in Houston, this piece is not for sale.

Also in the hallway hangs a hand cut from thick paper and brightly painted—reds, yellows, blues and greens, primary colors that remind us of our first pack of crayons. The title: *Hand*. This image, roughly six times the size of an adult hand, has a map of lines on the palm. The fingers are numbered 1 through 4, and the thumb is numbered 5. What would a palm reader discover? She might read the lines as a lunatic's travails. She might need to bring out her Tarot cards or blow the dust off her crystal ball. Purchase price in 2006: yet another gift. Current price: a nonnegotiable $634,000. A steal for the hedge fund manager with untraceable inside knowledge in the financial market.

In my office hangs, in semi-dark, another DeLoss McGraw, also untitled, which features gouache images of a red triangle-shaped box, a purple ladder, an upside-down chair, a pair of two-tone shoes, a pair of arms, a cart with red-spoked wheels, and a poet leaning forward as if he were flying or falling. How do I know it's a poet? Below the image is my poem "Moving Away," a tender call to my older brother, Rick, to remember our lean years. I view this work daily; no, hourly; no, every ten or twenty minutes when I'm called to my office by the landline—telemarketers are relentless and often begin their prerecorded pitch with, "Hello, seniors!"

Here, in this 2-by-3-foot piece, we have further evidence that artists and poets go together. Purchase price in 1998: a gift. Current price: $725,300. Buyer—corporation or upstart techie in jeans and T-shirt—think of it as an investment, and as dues paid to the creative world.

When I do a soldierly about-face, my eyes brighten on another framed gift from overly generous McGraw, Christmas 2016. It's an 8½-by-11-inch watercolor sketch inspired by William Shakespeare and me—yes, Shakespeare *and* me. Several years ago, I took a line from the Bard and built my own poem upon that line. Before the creative impulse ended, I had over a hundred poems, all of which began with famous lines, such as "All that glitters is not gold," "Shall I compare thee to a summer's day?" and, "We are stuff . . . rounded by sleep." The book of poems, *You Kiss by th' Book*, is still available. I have lots of copies in the garage; Chronicle Books, the publisher, has even more copies in its much larger garage.

Most of the poems in *You Kiss by th' Book* are long, robust, bawdy, wise as Solomon, and teasingly romantic. DeLoss and I had plans to create an art book based on the poems from this collection. This proverb-length one, starting from *Othello* 1.1.63, caught his eye: "I will wear my heart upon my sleeve / And up this sleeve is a trick or two."

And what did my collaborator render on the page? A long, flowing sleeve done in yellow, with a red heart at the center, a white rabbit, and a pair of playing cards—the two of spades and the three of hearts. An errant blue drop is outside the subject. I appreciate the gift, but I may part with it if times get hard. Current price in Ireland: €132,000. In the United States: $147,000. Insured shipping is available. Note: this artwork was done on typing paper and, therefore, has bubbled in places.

I sigh as I come to the end of the McGraws and am nearly as ashen as that prime minister in *Victoria*.

It's all over, I think, *my artful excursion*. Then I remember the file next to the living trust, the one called "DeLoss." It contains ephemeral items such as postcards (with drawings), letters, a single strand of hair, catalogues, an essay written by me, and also, now in my quivering hands, two rare originals: gouache paintings on watercolor paper. In one, a boy beams his large moon-like face at the viewer; in the other, a boy in a striped shirt looks out the window while the moon with eyes and ruddy cheeks looks in. I admonish myself—why didn't I frame them earlier!

We have other art displayed on our walls too. We also have antique Japanese tansus, a few rare books, some one-of-a-kind prints and fine jewelry, and a wedding kimono purchased for my wife on our twenty-fifth wedding anniversary. For insurance purposes I should tally our valuables, lick the lead of a pencil and enter the value of each piece in a book that will be opened by our daughter upon our passing.

And my ghastly film on VHS cassette? After I crush it under the nearly bald tires of my car—light bulb here!—I'll send the shards to DeLoss McGraw. Although our collaboration on the Shakespeare project didn't pan out, maybe the sparks of a new idea will color his thoughts. He will pour the contents of my package onto his worktable and study them like a forensic specialist combing through debris. Under his breath, he'll wonder, "Now what do we have here?"

Poet-friendly McGraw could do something with the shards. Perhaps he could create ladders, houses, rocking horses, another Alice, another couple not unlike my wife and me, and moons—lots of moons—from those pieces of a crushed VHS cassette. I am certain that he would send me a shard creation, though I would insist that he permit me to pony up, for he has been so generous in the past! In a letter dated Friday, February 6, he writes, "I really mean this—don't buy my art. Save your hard-earned money. I will trade you. The trade could be more for the both of us—if we make a show." He knows that the imaginations of poets and artists are a naturally crazy fit.

As for *Victoria*, the series may go on for several more seasons. An audience exists for this sort of slow-moving history. The queen reigns, lives with (and without) Prince Albert, and obliviously walks in splendor beneath some of the finest artworks in her country. I realize that the art displayed in the series should be of its time or earlier. But think—just think—of a camera panning a palatial ballroom past a Constable and a Turner to a wall of out-of-era DeLoss McGraw paintings! This would stop the wine-sipping audiences on both sides of the Atlantic.

Now we're talking value! Mucho dinero. I could shred my living trust and—like a prince—live comfortably ever after.

SOME NOTES ON DEATH

SUZANNE LUMMIS

THE ONLY CONSCIOUS, flat-out lie I've told in recent memory
was this: " . . . a little past 60." And, of that, only two words comprised
the lie, "a little." I like that lie, though, and think I'll keep it, just that *one*.
(In our Age of Lies, if people everywhere would at least put a cap on the
number of lies they allow themselves, well . . . Reader, I'll let you finish
that sentence as you see fit.)

So, now that I am a little past 60, I'm, yes, obsessed with death. I am as
obsessed as I was at 50, at 40, at 29. I could say I can't remember a time when
I was not obsessed with death, but that'd be a lie. I remember. I was 7.

Before 7 I'd been 6 and devoted to *LIFE* magazine, one of the few
communiques that reached the ski-lodge from beyond our snowbound
world. We had no TV. I'd admire the fat, curving Seagram's 7 logo with the
monarch's crown on top, so golden and resplendent, and looked forward
to turning 7 so that I could cut it out, taking care to follow the outline. I
could've cut it out right then, but at 7 it would take on more meaning.

I turned 7, and this is all I remember of that year. I learned to read rather
well for my age, and to ski poorly. (This condition would be set for life, good

reader, bad athlete). At the two-room schoolhouse, Mrs. Reed who was *nice* was replaced by Mrs. Powers who was *strict*. Perhaps someone had decided we boys and girls needed to be whipped into shape to fight Communism. Year round, I made valentines with my boyfriend, who lived in one of the cubicle apartments above the tracks with the other trainshed kids whose fathers were engineers or mechanics. Steven DiCarlo. And my parents wondered why so many liquor ads had been removed from their subscription magazines. None of these elements are related—they're just scraps I've retained.

I didn't think much about death.

Then, I turned 8.

The summer of my 8th year, my parents, with me and my 3-year-old brother Jimmy, traveled down through Mexico in the family's old Plymouth. Together with my very earliest recollections, from Palermo, Sicily, then San Francisco—most particularly, the maniacal hysterics rising from mechanical "Laughing Sal" drifting up from Playland at the Beach and mingling with the foghorns—certain impressions from that summer contributed to a reservoir of exotica I shifted around in my head for the remainder of my childhood. And *exotic* is what they were. *Colorful* is what they were—against the backdrop of quiet snow with, here and there, exposed pine bark or the black of rolling creek water showing through.

We'd spent most of the summer at sea level in a rented bungalow, just one highway between us and the sea, and the beach of Mazatlán. Now, on our way back—making various stops and excursions—we'd attained a height, on a promontory, and were looking down at the sea. At least, I certainly was. Far below me. It's here the memory begins.

Understand, I was not sad, nor happy. Just neutral, calm. I looked down the descending cliff and realized for the first time my life was in my hands. I had no intention of ending my life, no desire to, but I could. And with that thought I saw, as Shakespeare said, as Hamlet said, in my *mind's eye*, my future like an invisible ribbon, looping and turning as if in a shifting wind, following a certain course, then curling away, rippling, making shapes. It seemed not in my mind after all, but in the *air* stretching out over the glittering, salt water and into the distance. I realized if I went over the edge, all that was destined to happen to me, and whatever effects I might impress on the world, my life, my future, that *ribbon*, would crackle, break and begin to dissolve. From invisible to nothing, from nothing to never had been.

What would remain? A body of wistfulness, though that was me, then, feeling wistful. I wonder now if I knew the word *wistful*. I likely did because it's a word either of my parents might have used. I do remember being aware that I'd had a precocious insight: life is a choice. Death is a choice. I didn't know the word precocious, but I knew that by some mysterious means I'd advanced beyond the preoccupations of Steven DiCarlo, who was primarily interested in trying to plant wet kisses on me in the back of the school bus. To my thinking, this bit of a leap offset, somewhat, the fact that I was bad at arithmetic. And it offered some consolation against my disappointment that Seagram's 7 whiskey (today owned by Coca-Cola) didn't have a large, elegant number for people who were 8.

But there's more—something else occurred, a prefiguring. Years later, I'd sort through this, trying to get the sequence right. *What came first?* A lion. A lion came . . . down from the hills? Were we ever near hills? Mexico has mountain lions, like the rest of North America—that checks out. *Pumas.* A lion had carried off a child. (Dragged more likely.) I pictured it incorrectly with a richly curling mane, like the stone lions at the entrance to Sutro Gardens near Ocean Beach. A lion had carried off a child. We were in a village, in a place for visitors to eat and sleep—not a "hotel." Outside, hammocks hung under leafy awnings. Or maybe that was a different place, another stop. I lay awake thinking about the lion, the village men who'd gone off into the night—this night—to kill the lion, and the child who'd died-by-lion.

I've looked for records of children killed by lions, but the closest I can find is an Elena Salzar, female, age 5. But that would've been years earlier and in a place whose name doesn't ring a bell.

Be that as it may, I have never, since the age of 8, *not* remembered that I'd lain awake and listened to the clattering of insomniac insects, with the knowledge that men had left the village to hunt what had hunted, kill what had killed. A child, always, in my mind, a girl—her destiny had rippled before her, then sparked, sparkled and dissolved. What remained was not wistfulness. Blood on the earth.

Of course, by then I knew about death. There'd been pets. A beloved parakeet had flown out the window and was understood to have dropped frozen from a tree limb its first night out. It was a sweet bird, but that death did not haunt my imagination.

The child had not held the choice of her own life and death in her hands. The lion held the child. Held her. For me, that was the first death.

Since that trip, I have been infected with a sense of mortality, particularly my own. And, evidently, Death has been thinking of me. I cannot count the number of times I thought I would die. No, might die. To see the train bearing down on your stalled vehicle, or to be inside a car that's pitching over the edge of a ravine, that's Knowing. If I'd "known," readers, you would not be reading this now.

Wait, I lied. I just counted. Six times. No, seven. I forgot about the Landers quake—that made raggedy moves under me when I was in the fourth floor of a building of unreinforced brick.

Since death's on the bill here, I'd like to mention the first time—that is, the first time that was not felt as an abstraction or an occurrence that had befallen someone else.

I was nearing the end of my first semester in college and in a car full of revelers. I didn't know these revelers well, and don't remember their names now, but I knew the driver well, Dale, who would later claim it was the other driver's fault. Me, I'd never know whose fault. When my head hit the ceiling above the backseat I felt, quite distinctly, the organs inside my body, especially my heart. My heart declared itself in my chest—size, shape and location—like a three-dimensional cut-out.

When I came down, the passenger door had opened wide into the night air. I was half in, half out, half sitting. The woman I'd met only that night lay on the ground, talking quietly to the men surrounding her, Dale, her friend, and the driver of the other car. Strangers milled around. Someone came to check on me, "Are you O.K.?" I opened my mouth to speak but no sound came from me. He returned to the others, "Susie's O.K." Later, another came over, maybe Dale, "Are you O.K.?" No sound came from me. No sound could.

He was about to leave when I wrapped my arms around myself, my soaked clothes, and held them out in the yellowing, thin light of the headlamps. He saw then what he couldn't against my black shirt, inside the dark—my fingers, across my open palms, and up my arms, *red*. "Oh! Susie's bleeding…."

For generations, poet professors and workshop leaders have introduced an axiom to their beginning students and reminded—sometimes more than once—their intermediate students. It's a cornerstone of strong writing, particularly the writing of poets. That night I enacted to its fullest, most triumphal expression, that piece of practical wisdom. *Show. Don't Tell.*

I was resourceful maybe, but not brave. I did a lot of terrified whining in the ambulance. At 18, I had not become the person I was meant to be. I'd hardly become anything. I did not want to die a nothing, never to learn what was in store for me, to be as swept from the annuls of humanity like that child, pierced and dragged away into the foliage, whose name doesn't even show up in Children in North America Killed by Lions.

No fatalities were recorded in Fresno in connection with that car crash, and none needed to be. Thirty-one primitive stitches ear to ear stopped my blood from flowing down the sides of my head and across my shoulders like a benediction.

Sometimes, some days, I think of that event and every year since seems like bonus time.

Shortly before we Lummises crossed the border back into the US, I wrote my first poem. For years, when asked, "So how did you become a poet?"

I credited the opiate effects of the plump, low-hanging moon, which made a singular impression on me that night. Only later did I begin to piece in other images, recollections, that had endured this long—a bright, inviting sea, an invisible ribbon, an invisible lion. Invisible to me, though not to its prey.

I hadn't planned it, but it seems a motif of invisibility has found its way into my musings, culminating with blood that didn't show up against my black attire. If it weren't now already long after midnight, maybe I could make something of that. At this hour, nothing comes to me, nothing outside the obvious—Death is invisible. And, invisible, it senses vulnerability, waits for the right moment. Invisible, it's been stalking us all our lives.

Ah, but our theme here's about death and *aging*. Now that some of us are a bit past 60, it might be time to start thinking about death. Oh good! I'll excel at that.

GHOST NOTES

LAURIE BLAUNER

IRREVOCABLE

Death is a skeleton riding a white horse (like love) holding a black and white flag. The Tarot card represents change, transformation, transition. My dead cat, Cyrus, and dead father are insertions then subtractions. They evolved from living creatures to memories to ideas to feelings. I hold on. The past is far away, starting to collect like dust on everything and colored by experience, death a comparison. Sometimes there is death and sometimes there is addition, a box of air, earth drifting round and round, voyaging senses. And then everything changes.

I have placed a barrier so that I don't have to think about my own death until it's imminent. I hope to be alive one moment and gone the next because I'm a worrier. I will step farther, going backwards, until I finally fall off the roof. The knowing is the most difficult.

My first experience of death was flushing my pet baby alligator down the toilet where I hoped he would be reunited with other alligators in the sewers. Now I am still questionable, unhinged. Death is in much that I write as renewal, a plot device, or the conclusion of a character. It makes the world feel paper-thin, the grazing of two different materials against one another. Yet people kill themselves in so many ways, relationships and situations that erupt until someone feels too much, even a sunless winter or a sad song with an opportunistic guitar, an endless cause, synchronization, someone who knows better but is weary and desires nothing.

I like being in a quiet room for a long time. It seems death-like in its own way, but it is the opposite, a coffin flourishing, rest kaleidoscoping. I need silence and time to write. My childlessness and difficulties and criticism of myself are symptoms.

Statistics on anyone's longevity are individual based on sex, race, current age, height, weight, fitness, life events (income, education, marital status, etc.) and lifestyle choices (consumption of tobacco or alcohol), but generally the average 65-year-old male can expect to live to 87 and female to 89.

Death is a shock, even when expected, a mistake, or the stealing of something that you had offered someone already at a low price. You return to your room, unlocking it, and find it empty. There is an industry to deal with the bodies. Saudade is described as the love that is left when the object of that love is gone, a cacophony of sound gone silent, still echoing. Even with people brought back to life, we don't know what happens to us in death. Religions try to explain death and the afterlife. People who died and returned to life generally describe a personal heaven or hell, but scientists say it's the brain box deprived of oxygen.

ABSENCE OF

I blame too much on outmoded bodies. Can't we evolve into more spiritual beings, straddling this world and whatever is next? A better house for our souls? For example, the Great Chain of Being is a hierarchical structure involving all life and matter, beginning with God and ending with stones and minerals. It was important in Elizabethan, Renaissance, and Enlightenment thought. Epigenesis is focused on the human mind as the center of creativity and development.

Components of death:
Ghosts, accumulating in a hat or elbow or moving pencils or chairs
Bones, reciting the names for what has been dismantled and left in the spaces between sky and earth
Dust, the past and the future
Memories that take us elsewhere

What happened to all that beauty with its cold hands? The soul could be what happens when we stop consuming uncertainty, a small, red rain inside a body.

What to remember: we are all dying a tiny bit every day and a gift-shaped space haunts a wall.

Remember to laugh although you were only asleep. Breathe in, then out.

GHOST NOTES

I see my dead cat again in his usual places, even though I'm taking care of an elderly stray. A ball of undisguised light crawling across a floor distracts, makes me think it's something living. I become attentive. It squeezes, condensing my heart less and less. I'm accustomed to his staccato ghost, summarizing the parts of his life that I knew. There's a certain kind of loneliness for an animal. I feel experimental. I dreamt I was having sex with my husband when a bird flew inside our bedroom and tangled itself irrevocably in my hair.

The bones curving around my shoulders ache. When my grandfather died, my back hurt as I tried to avoid my usually absent father and his girlfriend, who was my age, at the funeral. It was his father, with his gnarled heart, in the box that would slowly turn to dust. They wanted me to be with them in their car to the cemetery. But I wasn't interested in getting to know either one of them. Later the woman became his wife, then left him, and he found another. My father's heart failed him in the same way his own father's had except that my father was sitting and watching floating bodies in the background glow of a television. I was something to grasp and put aside and perhaps next in the familial line of having my heart disappoint me.

Too many artist friends have died aortically young, often from accidents or cancer. My writer friends have fared better, living longer. As I grow older my infirmities greet me primitively and rhetorically, a broken bone in my left foot, a lost fallopian tube, half my thyroid. I don't have anything chronic. I splurge forward.

      Me: A sea of words to entertain you?

      Death: Don't be lackadaisical.

      Me: How about some tea or lemon cake? You know I resemble several
          other people.

Death: A mood must come over me.

Me: Ignore me.

Death: Something doubtful in me just undoubted itself.

Me: How far back do we go?

Death, laughing: This is easy.

Death, seriously: What do you think?

Me: That I've known you all my life.

FINALLY, FIRST PERSON

The doctors told my husband's father that he had six months to live because of lung cancer and a sarcoma they had operated on and could no longer treat. They placed him with hospice services. Six months later Hospice told him, "Call us when you need us." It's been almost three years. He is a contentedly cheerful person who adores his wife, reading newspapers, and programming his multiple VCRs. He has not changed into someone else. He just became more of who he already was.

I'm reading another book by someone long dead. I enjoy art by people who are no longer living. Much of my furniture was made by someone in their prime sixty years ago.

The dead don't stay dead. They change our minds. We have conversations with them, imagine new situations, extrapolate since there are lots of rooms in our minds and lots of places to hide secrets. We argue.

The future:
airy shoes and warm autobiographical food
hair growing ungovernably
everyone else is correct about me
trading in my childhood for apples
my thoughts are today's implications
affectionate sexual reconstructions
my teeth are equivocal, unsure about staying
I have a mouthful of verdicts yet my pants wander
my feet have become inappropriate
bodies, like day becoming night, impress us

Oh Death,

You are funny. Oh so funny. We met at an outdoor party late one night, behind a tree where my boyfriend and I had disturbed tree leaves, ferns, flowers, grass, mingling them, making them into other shapes and then smearing our bodies with the mixture. Pain and pleasure tickled me when I rode him. Yes, I drank too much, swiveling away from the out-held arms of tall dark trees that said, We are inside out, repeatedly. I liked to run in the dark, trying to avoid odd, dangerous things licked by moonlight that reminded me of other humorous things. I was useable. Rocks viewing our awkwardness made me think of gods judging us. But we aren't sedentary stones. We move and giggle and die on our own. We calibrate ourselves and our wants and what we can and can't do. I did it. I died because the world was inside me too much. A joke: the difference between sex and death is that with death you do it alone and no one laughs at you. For me it's humorous, for you it's . . . .

"Ghost Notes" appears in Laurie Blauner's new memoir, *I Was One of My Memories*, the 2021 Hybrid/CNF Pank Book Award Winner.

ENTROPY

CHRISTOPHER BUCKLEY

I know that a great man is indifferent to life and death,
His body changing form, gone with the floating clouds.

—Su Tung-Po 1061

WHEN YOU LOOK out into the night, it's clear that we're threatened in every direction with silence—a deep nothing that awaits every one of us beyond language, logic, money, career accomplishment, metaphysical or astrophysical guesswork. More and more these days, I can hear it ebbing in steadily from between the stars.

To try, facing the inevitable, more imminent now than ever, to think . . . to see if experience—which you have more of now than ever before—adds up to anything close to clarity about meaning; to understand why we die and if our life has meant anything to ourselves and one another, is the reason to keep writing and responding to experience.

Writing is a way of working it out. E.M. Forster said something to the effect that, How do I know what I mean until I've written it? We continue to write because it is the essential way we understand, it is how we explain our lives to ourselves, and, if we are fortunate, to others who read and are interested in such an essential ontological question as we face the universe with the thread of time thinning out into the dark.

Most writers want to interpret the moment(s) we hold in our hands as we face the stars. The enormity of space/time confronts us any time we stop to think of the flash that is a human life bookended by the eternities of the past and future. Blaise Pascal in the seventeenth century said, "The eternal silence of these infinite spaces frightens me." He was looking pretty much at the same night sky as we do now. I find myself as frightened now as when I was 6 or 7 years old, for the same reasons. Everything in between went in a flicker it now seems . . . .

In referring to her hometown of Oakland earlier last century, Gertrude Stein said, "There is no there, there . . . " and that is one of the great reasons for writing anything, to reason out our chances: is there something, anything at all, after this? Is there a there, there, as the orthodox have it? For over forty years I have gone back and forth between faith and doubt on this subject in my work. Hundreds of poems and essays and I don't know if I have come any closer to a resolution one way or the other, but I keep trying to interpret experience and translate the small details of my life that either hint at transcendence, or that I hope hint at it.

I think we all want to keep on with our lives as long as possible, and writing is how we define ourselves and the purpose of/to our lives. In addition to these essential questions about which we hope something will be revealed through our efforts, there is the simple dedication to and enjoyment of art and craft; that goes almost without saying. If I had arrived on the planet with the voice of Pavarotti, I would be singing instead of writing. For most, love of language and song was a place we started from. There is no good reason, as I see, to quit—neither metaphysical quandary nor aesthetic pursuit. Why give up your life? Writing is largely who you are— no compelling reason to sit in a chair and just stare out the window or shop online. It's interesting to me that this question of Why write after 60? even comes up. Certainly this is ageism on someone's part or at least our response to it?

A few years back I'd retired from full-time teaching and was teaching a poetry workshop once a year for a university's college of creative studies.

In one class a young man asked why I was still publishing—his implication, as I took it, was once you had achieved a level of publication/success, why continue? He may have viewed publishing and writing as something very finite, and so why was I taking up space in the world of publishing that someone, he for instance, might need? Ageism again as I saw it. My answer to him was a shorter version of what precedes this paragraph. It didn't get through to him, but I think that was because he was a beginning student writer and did not have, as far as I could tell from his work and interest, the vocation of writing. Had he been working at the craft for very long and found himself invested in it, I seriously doubt he would have asked such a question. I assume this student had never seen the 1976 movie *Logan's Run*, a future world with no disease, no wars, in which everyone is young and beautiful. There's a catch, of course: Everyone who reaches the end of their 20s must participate in a public death match, and those trying to escape are hunted by black-jumpsuited cops.

You spend your life developing your skills and habits of thinking and responding to life and the questions attached to it, so why would you abandon them? You give up a good deal materially compared to those with similar, or often less, education, but that is rarely the problem. What comes to many of us is the aesthetic quandary . . . Am I writing as well as I did at 35 or 40 or 45? The hope is that we keep improving book to book, that "muscle-memory" allows us to go forward in a good or expanded direction. This notion came up in a response I gave in an interview a few years back when asked how I chose among various forms for poems; did I set out to write a prose poem or quatrains, etc. I gave the example from my 20s when I was a tennis teaching professional, that when playing in a match I was not thinking of fundamentals—the correct form for a backhand or half-volley; rather, I relied on muscle-memory from years of practice to execute the shot. Similarly, I always recall the story of golfer Jack Nicklaus winning a tournament toward the end of his playing days. On the final hole he was near the green but behind a small tree with a Y in its trunk. Go around it to get safely on the green and he would bogey and tie, hence a playoff; risk pitching through the Y directly at the pin and he had a good chance for birdie and the win, which he did. A rather ungenerous announcer interviewing him after the win said, Wow

Jack, that was a pretty lucky shot at 18! To which Jack replied, "Yes, the more I practice the luckier I get."

So we have to take heart, and while most of us are not going to Sweden to collect a Prize in Literature, we can look at many examples of the writers who kept writing well, improving even, all their lives. I especially think of poets Wislawa Szymborska, Milosz, Amichai, Seamus Heaney, and Neruda. And my favorite US poets Mary Oliver, James Wright, Charles Wright, and Gerald Stern all who wrote wonderfully through their 60s and beyond. Especially close to my heart and mind are Philip Levine and Peter Everwine; Levine wrote/published the National Book Award winner, *What Work Is* and the Pulitzer Prize winner, *The Simple Truth*, in his 60s. Everwine's last two books were arguably his strongest and most luminous: *Listening Long* and *Late*, 2013, and the posthumous, *Pulling the Invisible but Heavy Cart*, 2019, books published in his 70s and 80s respectively. Of my contemporaries, Dorianne Laux, Gary Young, Robert Wrigley, Mark Jarman, Christopher Howell, Gary Soto and there are many more examples of course, but these come readily to mind. Certainly these examples are inspiration for those of us who continue to work to understand our lives on this planet through our writing/art.

We all recall Yeats saying the two main subjects are sex and death, and so certainly as one continues working later in life the subject of death weighs more heavily on the mind and often brings a darker cast to the work, but it also gives meaning to the life we have lived and pushes us, I think, to try and make sense of loss relative to living, and often I find that this pressure sends me back to examine many events from earlier life, to try and understand them in the face of mortality. One of my favorite poets is Gerald Stern, a poet who received recognition much later in life and who has kept on writing wonderful books into his 90s. In "Stepping Out of Poetry" Stern poses that, in his 50s—after years and years of work and having finally received some recognition (*Lucky Life*, the Lamont Poetry Selection for 1977 was published by Houghton Mifflin)—he might trade it all in, if he could, to be young and ambitious again and working toward the life/the poems he'd finally attained:

What would you give for one of the old yellow streetcars
Rocking toward you again through the thick snow? . . .

Oh, what would you give to pick up your stack of books
And walk down the icy path in front of the library?

What would you give for your dream
To be as clear and simple as it was then . . .

Looking back later in life he finds the value in life that largely escaped him at the time.

I feel I'm enunciating the obvious here? Often in my work I'm looking up to stars, but where else am I going to find anything to explain light slipping like sand through the hourglass of space/time? The arrow of time moves, in only one direction—we all know that . . . . The Second Law of Thermodynamics states that energy/matter over time degenerates, hence the entropy that's built in to every one of our cells. We get more of a feel for it—the stardust loosening in our bones—after 60, and a little reading in science reminds us that, before we know it, we're scattered back to bosons, leptons, and quarks. The question seems to be whether we will know it, or not. Jim Harrison said, "If nothing happens, we won't know it."

You'd think there would be something embedded in the quantum scrum of things, in the apparently boundless subscript of space, in the iconography of dust, in the cosmic jambalaya that, with proper work and inquiry, would let us know. These are the kind of thoughts I have come to. Younger, in the disaffection of youth, I think I spent too much time complaining. I want to know things for as long as I can, and know more. What choices do we have left? What might we deduce or prove with spectrometers and the electromagnetic radiation code of elemental color? I want to know if there is any option to consciousness.

And, so far as the soul is concerned, have we been buying metaphysical derivatives, betting on celestial puts and options all along . . . certainly a question for those of us who survived Catholic school and the absolute proselytization of the nuns.

The past continues to replay in the dust-swirled cup of the brain—dust, held there, queued up, so we might have a subtext against the days running out, the temporary particulate of infinity, the frayed tableaus we keep praying to/writing about one way or another. Is there a held cosmic breath? Our atmosphere's unraveling—will the last spindrift atom lift off to become nothing again or recount the lost praises of creation.

Time's almost up—our cells waving a white flag since the first web-footed fish stepped out on the shore. But I'm staying with it, trying to unpuzzle whatever I can. No reason to give up our days, any trace of an ontological agenda that might help us face the dark, know where we are going, or not . . . . My job writing is to marshal my grey cells and make the best guesses I can past the ionosphere, past each breath lost. To try to make sense of things.

In Gerald Stern's last nonfiction book, *Death Watch: A View from the Tenth Decade*, Trinity University Press, 2017, he asks: "And what was I? A little dust that sang too much? A miracle to beat all others?" A great question from a great poet and writer. Bless him, as he still speaks for us.

MY OBJECTS OF AFFECTION

KATHARINE COLES

Death sets a Thing significant

—Emily Dickinson

ONE

My father died in my hands, or under them, laid on; also under the hands of my mother and brothers and nieces crowding his bed for his last hard breath. When I first heard his death rattle, three days earlier, I knew it from Victorian novels; it's a sound I will no longer have to conjure for myself, out of words on a page.

During the days he took to finish, we moved in and out of his room, going home to sleep and shower, bringing back his favorite carry-out to pair with wines he would have loved if he hadn't been too preoccupied to drink them. We told stories around his bed, weaving the man we had known back into time.

Then—it came suddenly—the seconds between breaths extended, until at last he stopped laboring and became, *to touch*, not himself but a body. Late February, 2020: we had no idea what he would save himself—us—by dying when he did, in a memory care unit that would be closed to visitors in under a month. While his body cooled, we milled at his bedside, unraveling awe into loose ends: hunger, boredom, a rising anxiety to move back into our lives—not yet, never the same. To be doing anything, we gathered his things: photos, books, banjo, flannel shirts, mathematical proofs my brother had taped to his door in place of the usual decorative wreath or plaque, now none of it his. Arms laden, at last we left his body, past all that, for the van to transport to the medical school for its last use.

Elsewhere, everywhere, Emily Dickinson asks, "Go we anywhere / Creation after this?"

The pandemic broke over us, and we shut ourselves in. The English poet Paul Munden, known also for his interesting distractions, tagged me on Facebook. For his "From Our Confinement" invitation, he asked ten friends each to post an image a day for ten days of the spaces in which we'd sequestered ourselves, then to tag a friend of our own each day to do the same.

The question: Where are you?

Which came to mean, With what?

> Books on books.
> Musical instruments on shelves, leaning against chairs, waiting to be
> plucked, blown, tickled.
> An antique spindle.
> Carved and painted masks,
> artifacts of obscure origin and meaning.

Andy in Winchester, Jen and Shane in Canberra, Alvin in Singapore, Jesse Lee in Uruguay—here in Salt Lake City Lisa posted carnival-bright folk art and Susan whimsical ceramic birds. Around the globe, writers and artists looked over rooms for compositions to set moods and say— what? Hiding artful messes, they delivered tight shots of corners and halls, doorways moodily lit.

From me, a sea fan, a sculpture of glass and light, a bronze statue of an ordinary man. My grandfather's ebony elephants with their tiny ivory tusks, acquired a century ago on the other side of the world. Arrayed across the top of my bookcases: my father's mandolin, lute, Spanish bandurria, keeping songs to themselves. Things I look at in place and time, remembering the dead. I wear their rings on my fingers, bangles at my pulse, brooches pinning my throat. They hover out of reach. As does the world. When will any of us go so far again?

Along with objects, all my photos included windows, which, my house being a glass shoebox, I could only use—

Here, at dawn, a snowy canyon emerging into view outside, and,
   reflected from the inside, a lit-up kitchen. In between, my
   barely discernable reflection—
A day later: my treadmill in its welter of cords, beyond which the
   same canyon greens suddenly out of snow into spring—
All day, my rooms filling with clouds and birds, deer, the occasional
   fox—
Becoming an inner life.

I willed my Keepsakes—Signed away
What portion of me be
Assignable—and then it was
There interposed a fly—

With Blue—Uncertain—Stumbling Buzz
Between the light—and me—

Dickinson's "I heard a Fly buzz" opens with a rattle, vibrating the whole
sensory self. Inside "the Room" and outside, it makes itself felt as presence
"Between the Heaves of Storm," the threshold from which the "I" of the
poem speaks.

   Not the threshold but the windowsill, where at poem's end the fly will
simultaneously emerge into visibility and erase vision, along with hearing,
all sense. In the poem's extended metaphor, Dickinson uses this confusion
of sense, and its obliteration, to think through the passage the body
undertakes to become, like all things, subject to possession.

   "I willed my keepsakes," she says, "Signed away/What portion of me
be/ . . . ." Suspended in the line break between "be" and "Assignable,"
she elides the question of what "Assignable" objects may be left by will,
suggesting instead that she is "sign[ing] away" what of her will remain
here after death. Yet the body, as a rule, occupies a different category
than "Keepsakes"—except maybe in its nonperishable bits, a lock of hair
braided or the bleached finger bone of a saint; or unless, like my father,
this speaker donates herself to science, to be parsed and weighed, studied
and quizzed. As the body is at last dismantled and returned, its speaker's
earthly "Keepsakes," in their passage from her possession to the possession

of others, in time become not only all that can be kept of her, but at last all there is, the only "portion of [her]" that anymore "may be."

After that line break on "be," which places us into paradox, the poem falters in its strict rhythm, first forcing by means of the insistent iamb a hard stress from the last syllable of "Assignable," which in ordinary speech wants to be half-swallowed. Here, it can't be, since it's followed by the marked hesitation of "—and," which cannot bear weight so at once forces the stress backward to "ble" and shifts us emphatically along to the "then" that follows.

Thus, the act of assignment itself brings on the poem's anticipated end and closes its temporal circle: "And *then* it was" (my italics)—the precise moment in which presence becomes past—"There interposed a fly." In reintroducing from the beginning the "Blue—Uncertain—Stumbling Buzz" it seems also to enact, the line marks the final turn of the poem, where hearing gives way to sight. Between them, the windows and the eyes create the space in which the fly's "interpos[ition]" occurs. If before the fly existed sonically both inside and outside the body, now it comes visually "Between the light and me," "me" being the self as a whole and not merely its eyes, which the poem is careful not to name here; where the poem does name the eyes, back at the beginning of stanza two, they appear not as instruments of the speaker's vision, but as outlets "wrung dry" of the grief of others.

If a window can't "fail" in the way a body can, the fly interferes with the light at the whole site of presence. In its final line, "I could not see to see," the poem through repetition substitutes understanding for physical vision, distinguishing them in the moment of their mutual failure. I take this action of vision and its failure literally, physiologically. As the eye communicates back into the brain, so the brain reaches itself outward into the eyes, the connection between the two intimate and material. We look not at or through but with our visual apparatus, however unpalpable, even speculative, our nervous systems make our looking—by which I mean that unless something goes wrong, the eyes in their seeing feel like nothing, enabling presence without our noticing them. But acting as the transparent boundary between interior self and the world out there, they are anything but nothing.

The magic of the artifact: the thing touched by, made by, even once part of another's body: you can see this poem *in her own hand*, we say, by which I mean online, where I often visit it. The first time Google landed me on the Emily Dickinson Archive, a joint project of various holders of the original manuscripts, and I called up the handwritten version of "Long years apart," my body fizzed. Encountering *The Gorgeous Nothings*, the coffee-table-sized edition of Dickinson's envelope poems in, yes, gorgeous facsimile, my students, who can barely read handwriting any more, experience how Dickinson's hand, enacting a mind not regularized by a print medium that couldn't accommodate it, sets the poems free. None of this compares to being present with the actual pieces of paper on which Dickinson's own hand-penciled words still move across pages I once, in person, leaned over a glass case to decipher.

She was writing for the future. In her pockets pencils nestled with scraps of paper she reached her hand to find. As she made her poems, she wore them. They walked through the day with her, secreted in her famous, misunderstood white dress.

TWO

My California friend, whom I believe I see in my mind in both her younger and her fairly recent selves, claims to have the capacity neither to store visual memories nor to make images in her mind. When I finally see her again, though she will not look exactly as I picture her, I will know her, and she me. How does she recognize me (though not this terrible year, or next) across a huge conference center or on a crowded street, if she has no image in mind?

You might say she has no capacity to *imagine*, but my friend writes musical, vivid narrative prose, in which characters and objects come alive in surroundings that also come alive. I remember powerfully across thirty years one of her characters emerging into an unexpected flush, can still see the blushing, almost overripe loosening of her body, that object, as desire hardened. From an essay my friend sent me this spring, I carry a river, an inner tube, an adolescent girl riding downstream past a man on shore, who, as she drifts by, man-handles his own eye-riveting thing, which I see. People, objects, landscape: whatever my friend did or did not visualize in her head as she wrote—nothing, she claims—she doesn't need to see them. She has only to name them to lock me into a narrative stream.

In a fit of abstraction, Anne Carson says, "When the mind reaches out to know, the space of desire opens and a necessary fiction transpires" (*Eros*, 171).

Of an apple left high in an otherwise bare tree in Longus's novel *Daphnis and Chloe*, she writes, "The apple flies while standing still" (*Eros*, 89).

Flies *away*, I think, seeing that apple, apple-red in my mind's eye, though this is not what Carson says. The distance between me and the apple remains the same, but it seems to increase with desire.

Carson's translation of Sappho's fragment 105A goes,

> as the sweetapple reddens on the high branch
> > high on the highest branch and the applepickers forgot—
> no, not forgot; were unable to reach. (*Winter*, 215)

The apple I see remains unfixed and mutable, personal and idiosyncratic. Different from all others, maybe only mine gets away.

More poets than we think intentionally stinge on imagery—Dickinson, too, for whom "Hope is *the thing* with feathers" (my emphasis). I don't get to see the world lying outside Dickinson's failing windows, its theoretical apple tree and single unpicked apple, or on how high a branch that apple flies, overtaking what feathered thing. Nor does she show me what keepsakes domesticate her poem's room's interior, though I may bring to mind an image of the actual room in Amherst where her pockets hang for pilgrims to visit. Even her fly brings no visible self but all-encompassing darkness, a field of vision narrowing while "the space of desire," and the "necessary fiction" that arises in it, are foreclosed.

Not that Dickinson eschews imagery when she needs it—think of that "narrow Fellow," whose "Zero at the Bone" depends on our seeing, riveted, "the Grass divid[ing] as with a Comb," but any constructed presence relies on the rhetoric and requirements of the poem.

In an expediency of naming, "To make a prairie," composes its brief self, a kind of instruction manual, like this:

> To make a prairie it takes
> A clover and one bee,
> One clover and a bee,—

And revery.
The revery alone will do
If bees are few.

Of this, an imagination (the poem's colloquial "it," inhabited perhaps by a god but certainly by the poet, exerting omnipotence) begins by creating, in mind, an entire prairie, then (focusing down? scaling back? reversing time?) removes that prairie, leaving merely "a clover and one bee," one of each, no more. How delicate she is with her articles, and playful. The reversal —"one clover and a bee"—becomes not repetition but substitution, asking us to linger on difference in sameness. As with metaphor, the substitution of one thing for another not-quite-the-same thing opens space in the poem, not moving the reader forward but sending her back, then forth, then back again, to consider distinctions.

There's not a single descriptor in the poem. If you see a clover and bee, you've let their names suggest (or not, in my friend's case) pictures your own visual cortex supplies, lighting up exactly as if the objects appear before your eyes. The poem creates not imagery but a conceptual act, a movement of the mind.

Meanwhile, the distance between "one clover and a bee" on the one hand and "a prairie" on the other blows open Anne Carson's "space of desire" for me to inhabit, and you, dizzy and in motion, as does the distance between the reaching hand and the apple, which we fill with our selves. The poem becomes "the action of reaching out toward a meaning not yet known" (*Eros*, 166), perhaps not to be known.

Knowledge, like meaning, is hardly the point. If the poem means to tell me how "to make a prairie," the instructions couldn't be simpler. But Dickinson, a serious botanist, would have known they couldn't succeed, whether to make *your* prairie you're counting on propagation through seed, in which case you need at least two clovers, or through root spread, in which case the bee is superfluous.

Either way, "it takes" near enough forever.

When I think of my father these days, I almost always picture him outside, often eating—sitting on a restaurant patio or the long veranda of my now-sold childhood home, or high in the Wind Rivers range, perched on a rock beside a glacier-fed lake, with a chunk of salami in one hand and a pocketknife in the other. He will use the tip of the knife to winkle a smoked oyster from among its fellows, bedded in their rectangular tin; he will toss me an orange, and I will fail to catch it, as usual paying attention not to the fruit that flies toward me but to the one that escapes. Light glints on the lake, wind moves the trees, a cloud shreds its weather over high peaks. My father can see trout glimmering just under the lake's surface; equations hum in his head the way sentences hum in mine, different grammars rearranging the world's furniture, making order or its opposite. I smell the spices in the salami, the oyster's musky oil, the clean sharp orange peel when he breaks it for me. I can smell the rock, knowing as I do that these are not his memories, or even mine, but only words.

The plaid flannel shirt I took from his last closet is one of many I gave him—a "really good shirt," he said, which, over many washings, even as it softened, kept its bright ground, the color of an apple flying not on a branch but in the mind's eye. Far too big for me (he was over six foot; I'm not much over five), the shirt is good to throw over a T-shirt on a cold night. I imagine I smell him in its weave.

Maybe he pictured one of his sons in it, if he imagined anything during his last diminishing year. "Assign" our "portions" as we wish, we can't control where they go. I've gazed, only online, at Dickinson's vivid curl, now owned by Amherst College, which received it from the descendants of her lifelong friend Emily Fowler (Ford). At 23, Dickinson wrote to her friend, "I shall never give you anything again that will be half so full of sunshine as this wee lock of hair, but I wish no hue more sombre [sic] might ever fall to you" (*Ford*, #99).

According to journalist Steven Slosberg, two other locks listed as Dickinson's were left in the estate of the poet J.D. McClatchy. They are of different shades, only one the auburn she was known for in youth, but whose hair keeps its vibrance? Together, they sold at auction for $800, despite the uncertainties of their provenance, or because of them. The locks came to McClatchy on the death of his friend, James Merrill. Nobody is saying for sure how Merrill got them, but when Slosberg inquired of Langdon Hammer, author of the 2015 biography *James Merrill: Life and Art*, Hammer wrote back with a tale about a burglary. "[Merrill] said he took, if memory serves, a sherry glass—in honor of her eyes (which she described as sherry-colored). I assumed," Hammer writes, "this was an apocryphal story. But the Dickinson scholar Ralph Franklin suspects JM did in fact break in—perhaps to the Gables? Dickinson's brother-in-law's house. How else to explain the copy of Dickinson's poems inscribed to her sister-in-law Susan Gilbert, if memory serves, which was in JM's collection, and later donated by Sandy to the Beinecke."

Sherry glasses. Sherry-colored eyes. Confused relations and a book inscribed—by whom, since Dickinson herself was dead before any collection of her poems came out?—to the woman she may have loved above all others, to whom she wrote frequent passionate letters, though Susan lived next-door. Light as apples, her letters, ornamented with her barely legible hand; light and strong as birds, the hand-stitched fascicles; winged and abuzz, the poems she wrote on used envelopes: her script curving around flaps and addresses, the occasional whimsy of an additional fragment pinned on.

THREE

Since the virus came, except when I'm running or out gathering food, I find myself inside my glass box, spinning with things through space. "Now is a gift of the gods and an access into reality" (*Eros*, 153), Anne Carson tells us, though just at the moment, in our endless indoor wheel-spinning through the present, I find it difficult to believe her.

To Dickinson, bees are never superfluous. Nothing is, especially not *now*. She never meant me "to make a prairie," least of all in our lifetimes.

Maybe when she wrote she imagined someone like my father, who, when I was a child, planted trees that now tower over the neighborhood. Even when those trees had grown to the eaves, he decided the beech was a little too close to the house, so grabbed his shovel and drove his truck onto the lawn, full of purpose and joy— not to remove the tree, but to move it a few feet over—drawing the neighbors out to watch and comment.

Dickinson may have meant him, or me, or someone else in this future she either could or couldn't have imagined, to make or read a poem. Likely, she didn't care what any of us might do.

Except that when her sister threw open the trunk, looking for Emily's letters to burn as instructed, she found, to her astonishment, almost 2000 poems. Which, Emily not having mentioned them in her instructions, Lavinia had the sense not to burn.

Like the poet, a bee works again over her blossom, gathering and stuffing her little thigh-pouches until it seems impossible she might still fly. The blossom yields, and between bee and flower I am carried away, flying at once like an apple leaving orbit and like a bee loaded down. The poem has found and instructed me, not in agri- or apiculture but in "revery," the making of a dream of clover over which a bee in her singular resonant multitude browses, as do I. Conjured objects, and revered— clover, apple, bee—release me into the dreaming field of poetry. This is the poem's instruction.

For years, I assumed Dickinson's clover flowers were pinkish-white, like those I see in my yard. But prairie clover is gorgeously purple, which my father, being more like her than I, would have known. The poem doesn't care either way. You don't have to *see* any of it. Rather, Dickinson depends on your apprehending.

Dickinson eludes us because she means to.

"Neither for me honey nor the honey bee," says Carson's Sappho (*Winter*, 146). And yet, between them, Sappho and Carson, like Dickinson, give us both.

The objects are everything. And, like so many things, also beside the point.

Aside from his red flannel shirt, the things I received from my father came before he died, though after he had begun his long passing away. When he went into care, my mother sold the family home and its veranda, its high ceilings and commensurately long staircases, including the wooden one, polished to a treacherous shine and bottoming out at a bone-cracking marble floor. What she didn't take with her to her new condo she offered to her children. What we didn't want, and a few things we did, she gave away or sold.

I had no use for my father's hunting rifles or place for the excellent canoe my mother bought him one birthday. His little bits of jewelry and cashmere sweaters, which like his best wines he saved for festive occasions, went to my brothers, the cellar to my mother, who shares it with her children a few bottles at a time.

My father never collected ornaments and baubles, though I happily wear my great-grandmother's passed-down jewels with jeans and flannel, as if they are meant for real life. He liked good things he could use: bungie cords, binoculars, trucks with the power to uproot mature trees; the Mojo Pizza ballcap my older brother brought him from Phoenix, or the one I carried back from Palmer Station in Antarctica, which let him bear an applique of a frozen continent like a hood ornament on his forehead. A fan of magpies, a Depression baby, my father repurposed yogurt containers and collected used twist-ties, tinfoil re-smoothed and folded away in a drawer. He might say of a paper sack that looked binnable but whose structural integrity he'd assessed at a touch, "That's a really good bag." When his children made fun of him, he would put his serious face on over the satirical one and say, "In the next war, you'll beg me for rubber bands."

The pandemic arrives, keeps arriving.

"Like a face crossing a mirror at the back of the room, Eros moves," Anne Carson tells us. "You reach. Eros is gone" (*Eros*, 166).

After he died, people told me things I wished I'd always known. He had taught my mother to see animals secreted, invisibly to others, in their environments: fawns left safely nestled among leaves (my father could smell them, she says); leaf-shaped birds sheltering in the trees. Sitting in a winter clearing high in the Uintahs, he hushed an old friend so they could listen to snowflakes crackling. I have their stories and my own that, like some objects, keep coming to mind. I mean "come" in the sense of lift, into clarity, into semblance and resonance, into flight.

Carson says, "In any act of thinking the mind must reach across this space between known and unknown, linking one to the other but also keeping visible their difference" (*Eros*, 171).

Go we anywhere? I wonder now if I should have taken a lock of hair, clippings from his fingernails. It would have been unlike me a year ago, but now, so many of us having slipped alone into memory, I might become someone who would wear a remnant of my dead father around my neck.

"The tie between us is very fine," Dickinson wrote to Susan Gilbert, "but a hair never dissolves" (*Gilbert*, #HB148).

At night, the bright outside fades from my rooms. My house, its

ghostly interior reflected on itself again and again, overflows its objects.
The body I hardly notice any more glimmers faintly by.

"My Objects of Affection" appears in Katharine Coles's latest collection of essays,
The Stranger I Become: On Walking, Looking, and Writing; Turtle Point Press, June 2021.

WORKS CITED

Carson, Anne. *Eros the Bittersweet.* Dalkey Archive Press, New York, 1998.

Carson, Anne, translator. *If Not Winter: Fragments of Sappho.* Vintage, New York, 2013.

Dickinson, Emily. "I heard a fly buzz – when I died." F591A/J465. *Emily Dickinson Archives.*
https://www.edickinson.org/editions/1/image_sets/235826. Transcribed by author.

———. "To make a prairie." J1755/F1779. *The Poems of Emily Dickinson.* Ralph W. Franklin, ed.
Cambridge, The Belnap Press, 1998. Text first published 1896, Todd and Bianci series.

———. Letter to Emily Fowler Ford, *Dickinson/Ford Correspondence.* http://archive.
emilydickinson.org/correspondence/ford/l99.html.

———. Letter to Susan Gilbert. Correspondence with Susan Gilbert. http://archive.
emilydickinson.org/working/zhb148b.htm.

Slosberg, Steven. "The Bewildering Provenance of Emily Dickinson's Auburn Locks."
The Westerly Sun, May 25, 2019. https://www.thewesterlysun.com/opinion/guest-
columns/postscripts-the-bewildering-provenance-of-emily-dickinson-s-auburn-locks/
article_4704226e-7eb5-11e9-9e9c-dfc674af5052.html

WHEN I AM TRULY COMPLETE

BONNIE SUMMERS

MINUTES go by so fast I can hardly keep track of even just the highlights, rarely make sense of them before new ones come. Thoughts and conversations overlapping sounds, smells, sights, insights, waves of feelings, surprises all keep coming, why so quickly? Life is lovely, rich, complex and mine. At the end of it all I had hoped to have a full record of my existence within it, you know, proof I have been here, a puzzle finished, all the bits and pieces in place. Wanted to look at it carefully myself, the whole picture. I'm doing the best I can to catch it with my fast-flowing pen, plenty of paper, people who kindly tolerate my eccentric use of time, but at my last chapter, when I'm becoming truly complete, who will write *that* ending part down, as my hands and throat crave rest, yet still I work to understand my living while dying? How can my last sparks turn into black and white, ink on page? Who will jot down what I see as my breath shallows and slows, how I feel not feeling anything (and not because I'm distracted or numb), make notes when everything turns dark for good, record how I feel as I'm buried or cremated and scattered? Who will report how it is for me not to look back just one more time, not to have another chance, to run out of time for the next question and its answers, not to be able to use what I learn from these last moments, to never say what I really intended—later on, when I've thought it over and can let my meaning show unmistakable in my eyes? Who will write down how it is for me to simply stop being, as I know it, how it is to return to the comfort of ashes, *that's* what *I* want to know, who will write all that? Who?

SUMMER'S LEASE

SUSAN TERRIS

I rise and fall, and time folds
Into a long moment . . .

— Theodore Roethke, "Journey to the Interior"

AS EAGLES SCOUR winds of morning, cleat-clink on the flagpole
and a cell phone in the lake. Not a day from the past, one of those lost
idylls with shovel and pail and bleached snail shells as I made sand cookies,
taught careless minnows to do the backstroke. Still, watch for the small
girl on the dock. In yellow-green water, you'll lose sight of a dropped
fishing pole and spread-eagled child. Below the mocking surface, who
is she, who was she? If I dig in the sand until water comes up, will my
younger face, reflect up from that shallow pool?

Nearby, in Itasca, where the mighty Mississippi begins to flow, in Itasca
which isn't even a Chippewa or Ojibway word but scholar-coined—from
Latin, no less, *veritas caput*: the true head. *Caput*, the head, my head stores
all myths true or false. Here, 2,552 miles above the Gulf of Mexico, I
drop a twig in the river. A child wades, watches the twig, crosses the log
bridge between yesterday and today. Yesterday, I was that child. See her,
brown fawn of a girl, eager to slip undetected among the cattails. Or dive
down into this river or the lake. Find a sunken timber from more than
a hundred years ago. Yes, look—there in a faded, blue tank suit, another
girl sits reading *Anna Karenina*, unaware of the deep water cradling her.

Shadow of wolf and coyote above, shadow of satiny skin time will warp and stretch.

That night, there's a moonbow. Not the rabbit or frog in the moon and not the man either. But the girl? Who is she now? How to speak about loss and about a body grown past the sun, one better seen now in the shades of night as a flickering bow arches over the lake, offering—what?—a sky message, one that says never-say-never, never apologize for age or for the ripple of old flesh. You see, for me, this is the place of all ages yet none. Here I am girl, mother, grandmother, and—yes—great grandmother, too, as I paddle my kayak into the prismatic path of the moon.

Tomorrow I may even be the shadow in the shadow as cumulous slowly bandages blue. The wind will be cold. Tomorrow I'll tell northbound geese they are wrong-headed, warn bear and turtle to think about shelter. North is the way to winter. North, like *veritas*, is the white within white. Last year, my mother's best friend died alone in her cabin. Her picture, in a boat-shaped frame, sits on what was my mother's desk, as I still live my arc of a life, rounded, turning, puzzled, deer tracks hard to follow in the shade. White-capped surface of the lake is shook foil in the sun, as the head of an eagle—who preens on a branch above slapping water—dazzles. No eagles when I was a girl, no fear of the never-again. Only fear of what-if and ever.

O, song of the flagpole, sonata of wave and wind, out by the sandbar, in the shallows, wild rice grows. Move toward it, wait, listen. River or lake: watch twig and wing. Keep on bringing water and light. But please don't try to tell me the lease is almost up.

SORTING AND STACKING
IN THE STONE GARDEN

SHARMAN APT RUSSELL

IN THE 1960s, the divorced 58-year-old Hazel Iona Stiles moved to the
Mojave Desert of southern California. She was drawn by a late and loopy
Homesteading Act in which "settlers" were given five acres if they "proved
up" by building a small house. Few of these parcels had access to water,
electricity, or a paved road—a model of how not to develop land. One
of Hazel's three sons later visited her and found her new home "not really
livable," but she seemed happy enough in that small house, supplemented
by a smaller trailer, buying her water in bottles, using kerosene lamps, and
pursuing the spiritual themes that interested her.

Hazel studied metaphysics and a Christian Science philosophy that
emphasized the equality of women, the importance of prayer, and the
illusion of the material world. The Creation of God was made of spirit,
not matter. Life was love. Love was eternal. Eventually, Hazel began to sort
and stack rocks, painting some in primary colors, red, yellow, and blue,
others with a single pink or orange dot. Over time, she made thousands of
trips into the nearby hills, collecting more rocks and placing them just so
on her proved-up five acres.

She was spelling out words, big words about my height, most
prominently GOD BLESS AMERICA, CALIFORNIA, AND OUR
WORLD. And somewhat smaller words, SEEK PEACE, PURSUE

PEACE, WORK FOR PEACE. She quoted from Shakespeare: "Sweet are the uses of adversity, which like the toad ugly and venomous wears yet a precious jewel in his head, and this our life exempt from public haunt, FINDS TONGUES IN TREES, BOOKS IN THE RUNNING BROOKS, SERMONS IN STONE, AND GOOD IN EVERYTHING." She also gave her own good advice. SING, DANCE, PRAY, TURN OFF TV. Neighbors from the nearest five acres would sometime see her bending, lifting, arranging. "She was always working so hard," one said to me, although he never knew what she was working at.

Hazel worked until she couldn't and spent her last years in a nursing home. She died at the age of ninety-nine. Some years after her death, a man retired to the same loopy desert area, still an unincorporated community called Wonder Valley. Disabled by a neurological disease, the man took up drone photography, sending himself spiritually out into the world. Soon he was seeing words in the desert. TONGUES. SERMONS. PEACE. One thing led to another, and today I am here before the wreckage of Hazel Iona Stile's squat mucous-colored house, accompanied by a volunteer from an organization that would like to protect her stone garden. Without this man, I would never, ever have found this homestead surrounded by desert in a maze of dirt roads that lead to other homesteads, often enough abandoned houses like this one.

Shingles litter the ground, parts of walls, windows, doors, leakage everywhere. "Be careful," the volunteer says before taking me inside to another unholy mess, scattered pages from books, scattered books, the kindling of old furniture, mouse and rat droppings, fast food bags from transient squatters. It's the mess we are always leaving behind. Through a hole in the wall, I can see Hazel's trailer turned upside down. "That was the wind," the volunteer explains. Wonder Valley is known for its ferocious wind.

In Hazel's stone garden, though, the wind has improved her work, the sermons scraped clean of paint, brown like the mountains and hills, sand and gravel, words and desert one and the same. I go ahead of the volunteer, careful to keep to the narrow path between the bursts of celebration, FIND TONGUES IN TREES, AND GOOD IN EVERYTHING, many of these trails lined with smaller rocks and following the subtle contours of land.

I think but do not say to the volunteer that this is about me, too, these words exposed to wind, unseen, unimportant except for the effort and emotion they represent. I've been a writer almost all my life, and it was always like this, spending your time sorting and stacking, working hard, happy in the doing. Just doing writing was good enough.

I believe I was careful. I believe I never chose writing over my children or husband or teaching responsibilities or exercise or lunch with friends. I chose, above all, a balanced life and disapproved of artists who aggrandized their art. My heroes were not writers but third-grade schoolteachers, environmental activists, and people who got out the vote. I only nodded, cleared my throat, when passionate writing students said "the world needs this story" about their story. I didn't think the world needed our stories so much as we needed to tell them.

As for myself, I wrote all the time, in the crevices, early in the morning, on the weekends, on a plane, hardly ever for long stretches—that wasn't possible with children and husband and jobs and friends—but steady, steady, steady, committed to one book while planning out the next. This discipline resulted in twelve published books in thirty years. One day I had an insight, which I shared with those passionate writing students, "I always thought writing would get me closer to the truth. Sometimes, though, I wonder if it's getting in the way."

Now, at the age of 65, I have roughly ten minutes to thirty-five more years. Let's just say the last leg of the trip. The question for so many of us remains: what do we want to do with the rest of our lives?

I want to die well. By this I mean the achievement of inner peace, preferably a few hours bathed in love and acceptance, grateful and gracious. "She died so well!" the audience that lives in my head will say. "She was radiant, absolutely radiant!" I want to die in control of my childhood selves and also, perhaps unique to my generation, I want to resolve that desperate feeling about the state of the world, my own guilt and complicity, the promise and failure of being human on this beautiful Earth. "What a great ending!" the crowd will murmur, wandering from the dissolving theatre into shivery blackness and glitter of stars. "Such a sense of hope."

I am more aware than ever that writing may not be the path to these resolutions. To be honest, probably is not the path. My time would be better spent doing insight meditation and hallucinogens. I really should manage the plastic in my life. Participate in a climate change march. Of course, writing does not preclude these activities. Let me say right here: I hope to do them still.

But what I have come to understand is that I have no desire to write less in the next ten minutes or thirty-five years. I am not going to prioritize mindfulness or even politics. After family and friends, I am going to prioritize writing. I am going to write as many more books as I can! Say it loud, say it proud. I'll die with my boots on. Something drives me. Something is having too much fun. Something still thinks—writing about that would be hard to do. That's a weird and knotty thing to write about. I think I'll try.

I have a theory about experiential mysticism. Talk about aggrandizement. In this theory, in our best act of writing, every word, every semicolon, every plot twist, every dialogue, every bit of research and humor is part of the larger whole—the essay or story or poem. We are trying to create a world in which all the parts are connected, and all the parts are important. Revision is crucial in this process, shaping and pruning, adding, subtracting. We build these worlds and ecologies, and that's exciting—to be the builder and creator—even as we are aware of the humblest comma or pronoun reference. Nothing is careless or separate or alone. In doing this, we are not in our ordinary selves. We are another, larger self who is standing apart, shaping in mimicry or reflection of what both the mystics and the scientists say: All in One, One in All.

I often write about science, an attempt to reduce complex subjects to emotional terms, and I am fond of scientific papers which perform the opposite trick, reducing emotional subjects to complex analysis. In "Brain Activity and Connectivity During Poetry Composition," published a few years ago in a journal hitherto unknown to me, *Human Brain Mapping*, scientists did PET scans of both expert and novice poets as they wrote poems and then as they revised poems.

For both phases of creativity, the part of the brain that motivates was highly engaged.

During the generation or first draft of a poem, however, cognitive control—self-monitoring, suppression of irrelevant stimuli, manipulation of information in working memory, and other aspects of focused attention—was distinctly disengaged. Critical judgments were suspended and remote associations encouraged.

During a revision of the poem, that cognitive control started up again.

Writers already know this. Still, the actual scans are startling. Specific parts of the brain light up during generation and specific parts during revision, and all this seems to happen in the same parts of the brain for both new and experienced writers. Some differences did emerge. Poems in the scientific study were assessed for their quality and craft by an independent panel. And, yes, "When poems with high craft scores were generated, the MPFC [medial prefrontal cortex] was more strongly coupled to a set of language-related brain regions" and "more weakly correlated to the posterior parietal areas and pars opercularis." Writers know this, too. Writing is training and exercising not the pars opercularis (the motor aspect of speech) but the ability to couple and connect between distant parts of your brain. To race around your brain making connections.

This is all to say that writing is a physical activity and that, unlike Hazel Iona Stiles, I believe in matter as much as spirit, and perhaps more so. The ability to race around diminishes as we get older, and, of course, I may not die with my boots on at all. I may lose strength, too weakly correlated to generate high craft scores. I may lose speed, unable to reach those language-related brain regions in time.

I have a back-up plan, one which is related to Hazel's stone garden and nicely refers to the beginning of this essay. I won't be sorting and stacking rocks. That would be derivative. I want to collect small glittering pieces of tile—broken tile, glass bits, marbles, seashells, jewels, nanotechnology— and glue them to the inside walls of my house. I'm pretty sure I'll be fit enough to do this, spending a few hours every day with bright color, placing them just so in particular patterns, recycling little bits of our human world, creating pattern upon pattern so that you will be able to enter these rooms and sit surrounded by a pattern and color that forms a larger whole. I guess I'll need a ladder for the ceiling. Obviously, the biggest challenge will be when I run out rooms and need to spill out of the house. That could become an eyesore (I'm aware), but I'll work with the neighbors. I'll continue to be careful. The world won't need this. Only I will need to do this. Because it's in the doing.

I think that's okay.

EDITOR

KATHARINE HAAKE's most recent work is a chapbook of fabulist parables, *Assumptions We Might Make About the Postworld*. Her other books include an eco-dystopian science fiction fable, *The Time of Quarantine*; a hybrid California prose lyric, *That Water, Those Rocks*; and three collections of stories. Haake's fiction and nonfiction has appeared in such journals as *One Story*, *The Iowa Review*, *Crazyhorse*, *Witness*, *Alaska Quarterly Review*, *Fiction International*, and *Shenandoah*, and, among other distinctions, has been nominated for the Pushcart Prize and recognized as distinguished by *Best American Short Stories* and *Best American Essays*. One short story collection was a *New York Times* Notable Book; another was a *Los Angeles Times* Best Seller. A collaborative text/image diptych she did with artist Lisa Bloomfield is included in Bloomfield's portfolio in the permanent collection of the Los Angeles County Museum of Art. Haake is also a longtime contributor to the scholarship of creative writing theory and the author of the foundational text, *What Our Speech Disrupts: Feminism and Creative Writing Studies*. A recent fellow at the Djerassi/Leonardo Scientific Delirium Madness residency, Haake has also been awarded a Master Artist's Fellowship from the Cultural Affairs Department of the City of Los Angeles. She is a Professor of Creative Writing at California State University, Northridge.

COEDITOR

GAIL WRONSKY is the author, coauthor, or translator of fifteen books of poetry and prose, including the poetry collections *Under the Capsized Boat We Fly, New & Selected Poems*; *Imperfect Pastorals*; *Poems for Infidels*; and *Dying for Beauty*, a finalist for the Western Arts Federation Poetry Prize. She is the translator of Argentinean poet Alicia Partnoy's book *Fuegos Florales/ Flowering Fires*, winner of the American Poetry Prize from Settlement House Press. Her poems have appeared in many journals, including *Poetry, Boston Review, Antioch Review, Denver Quarterly, Poetry International, Guesthouse,* and *Volt*. She is the recipient of an Artists Fellowship from the California Arts Council. Her work has appeared in anthologies, including *Poets Against War*; *The Black Body*; *In Possession of Shakespeare*; *The Poet's Child*; and *Coiled Serpent: Poets Arising from the Cultural Quakes and Shifts of Los Angeles. The Moose in the Moon*, her book of poetry for children, was recently published by Tsehai Publishers. She teaches creative writing and women's literature at Loyola Marymount University where she was awarded the Harry M. Daum Professorship. She lives in Topanga, California.

CONTRIBUTORS

KIM ADDONIZIO is the author of several books of poetry and prose.
Her most recent poetry collection is *Now We're Getting Somewhere*,
from W.W. Norton. Her memoir-in-essays, *Bukowski in a Sundress*, was
published by Penguin. She has received fellowships from the NEA and
Guggenheim Foundation, Pushcart Prizes in both poetry and the essay,
and her work has been widely translated and anthologized. *Tell Me* was
a National Book Award Finalist in poetry. She lives in Oakland, CA.
www.kimaddonizio.com.

FRANK BIDART has been awarded the Pulitzer Prize for Poetry, the
Bollingen Prize, the Griffin Poetry Prize Lifetime Recognition Award, and
the National Book Award. His most recent book is *Half-light: Collected Poems
1965-2016*. He lives in Cambridge, Massachusetts.

PATRICK BIZZARO has published eleven books and chapbooks of
poetry, most recently *Against Confusion* from Mount Olive College Press and
Interruptions from Finishing Line Press. To Bizzaro's credit are two critical
studies of Fred Chappell's poetry and fiction with LSU Press, a book on the
pedagogy of academic creative writing with NCTE, four textbooks, and a
couple hundred poems, reviews and review essays in literary magazines.

He has won the Madeline Sadin Award from NYQ and Four Quarter's Poetry Prize as well as a Fulbright to visit South Africa during 2012. His co-edited book on poet and pedagogue Wendy Bishop, *Composing Ourselves as Writer-Teacher-Writers*, was published spring 2011 by Hampton Press.

LAURIE BLAUNER is the author of eight books of poetry and four novels. Her first book of hybrid nonfiction, *I Was One of My Memories*, which includes her essay here, won a 2021 PANK Book Award Contest. Her latest book of fiction is *The Solace of Monsters*; and a recent book of poetry, *A Theory for What Just Happened*, was published in early 2021. She lives in Seattle, Washington. Her website is www.laurieblauner.com.

CHRISTOPHER BUCKLEY's recent books are *Star Journal: Selected Poems*, University of Pittsburgh Press; *The Far Republics*, winner of the 2017 Vern Rutsala Poetry Prize, Cloudbank Books; *Chaos Theory*, Plume Editions; *Cloud Memoir: Selected Longer Poems*, Stephen F. Austin State University Press; *Agnostic*, Lynx House Press 2019; and *The Pre-Eternity of the World*, Stephen F. Austin, 2021. He has recently edited *The Long Embrace: Contemporary Poets on the Long Poems of Philip Levine*, Lynx House Press, 2020, and *Naming the Lost: The Fresno Poets—Interviews & Essays*, Stephen F. Austin State University Press, 2021.

ELENA KARINA BYRNE's publications include the chapbook *No Don't* (What Books Press, 2020); her fourth book of poetry, *If This Makes You Nervous* (Omnidawn, 2021); and work in *Pushcart Prize XXXIII*, *Best American Poetry*, *Poetry*, *The Paris Review*, *Poetry International*, *Plume*, *BOMB*, and elsewhere. Former Regional Director of the Poetry Society of America and Kate & Kingsley Tufts Poetry Awards judge, Elena is a private editor, lecturer, Poetry Consultant & Moderator for *The Los Angeles Times* Festival of Books and the Literary Programs Director for the Ruskin Art Club. Work in progress includes a collection of stories, screenplays, and essays called, *Voyeur Hour: Poetry, Art, Film, & Desire*.

KATHARINE COLES's books include seven collections of poems, most recently *Wayward* (Red Hen Press, 2019). Her memoir, *Look Both Ways*, was released in 2018 by Turtle Point Press, which will also publish *The Stranger*

I Become: On Walking, Looking, and Writing (essays) in 2021 and *Wouldn't Dream* (poems) in 2022. Poet-in-Residence at the Natural History Museum of Utah and the SLC Public Library for the Poets House FIELD WORK program, she has received awards from the NEA, the NEH, the NSF's Antarctic Artists and Writers Program, the Guggenheim Foundation. She is a Distinguished Professor at the University of Utah.

CATHRYN COLMAN's first book *Borrowed Dress* won the Felix Pollak Prize for Poetry and was on the *The Los Angeles Times* Bestseller List. Her second collection, *Beauty's Tattoo*, was published by Tebot Bach. Her latest book, *Time Crunch*, is out from What Books Press. She has won the Browning Award and the Asher Montandon Award, judged by Campbell McGrath. Her poetry has appeared in *The Colorado Review, Ploughshares, The Huffington Post, Gettysburg Review, Prairie Schooner, The Southern Review, Barrow Street, Writers on Writing* (Putnam), and elsewhere. She has been a free-lance reviewer for *The New York Times Book Review.*

MICHAEL C FORD's first CD, entitled *Fire Escapes*, was a 1995 entry from New Alliance Records & Tapes. Hen House Studios has been promoting and marketing his CD, *Look Each Other in the Ears* (2014.) That document (both vinyl and CD) features a stellar band of musicians not the least of which were surviving members of a 1960s theatre rock quartet that most of you may recall as The Doors. In 2015, a chapbook length poem, *The Driftwood Crucifix*, was published by Los Ranchos Press. In 2017, *Women under the Influence* was published on the Central Coast by Word Palace Press. Foothills Publishing in New York State offers a book-length collection entitled *The War Chamber Ministry*. His debut 12-inch-vinyl recording, *Language Commando*, earned a Grammy nomination on the 1st ballot in 1987, and his book of selected work, *Emergency Exits*, earned initial nomination for the Pulitzer Prize for poetry in 1998. *Populated Wilderness* is being published in a 2021 chapbook format as a fundraiser for Lockwood Animal Rescue Foundation.

MONA HOUGHTON has had stories published in *Carolina Quarterly, Crosscurrents, Bluff City, Write Launch*, and *Full Blede*, and an essay she wrote, "What I Learned from a Bricoleur," appeared in *Everyday Urbanism*, edited by Margaret Crawford and John Kaliski. Mona won the John Gardner Memorial

Prize for Fiction for her story "A Brother, Some Sex, and an Optic Nerve," which appeared in the 2010 Summer Issue of *Harpur Palate*. *Frottage & Even as We Speak—Two Novellas* was published by What Books Press in 2013. Mona taught creative writing at California State University, Northridge for many years.

MARK IRWIN is the author of ten collections of poetry, including *Shimmer* (2020), *A Passion According to Green* (2017), *American Urn: Selected Poems* (1987-2014), and *Bright Hunger* (2004). Recognition for his work includes The Nation/Discovery Award, two Colorado Book Awards, four Pushcart Prizes, the James Wright Poetry Award, the Philip Levine Prize for Poetry, and fellowships from the Fulbright, Lilly, and NEA.

RICHARD KATROVAS is the author of sixteen books of prose and verse from Wesleyan University Press, Carnegie Mellon University Press, and Louisiana State University Press, among others. He taught for twenty years at the University of New Orleans, and since 2002 at Western Michigan University. He's the founding director, and owner, of the Prague Summer Program, LLC. He's received numerous fellowships, grants, and awards, most recently the 2018 Gold Medal for Fiction from the Faulkner Society. The essay herein will appear in *Chained to a Tree: A Memoir in Essays about Poets and the Fools Who Love Them* from LSU Press.

RON KOERTGE is the current Poet Laureate of South Pasadena, CA. He has the usual array of prizes and publications.

MARTIN LINDAUER has published short fiction, essays, and memoirs, most recently in *Tikkun Magazine*. A retired professor, he has published widely on psychology and the arts, including *The Psychological Study of Literature* (1975, Nelson-Hall); *Aging, Creativity, and Art* (2003, Springer); *Psyche and the Literary Muses* (2009, John Benjamins); and most recently, *Mass-Produced Original Paintings, the Psychology of Art, and an Everyday Aesthetics* (2020, Palgrave Macmillan).

BRET LOTT is the author of fourteen books, the fifteenth—*Cherries on the Golan, Olives in Jerusalem*, a collection of essays on food and Israel and Palestine and hope—coming out in late 2021. He has spoken on Flannery

O'Connor at The White House, served as Fulbright Senior American Scholar and writer in residence at Bar-Ilan University, and for six years was a member of the National Council on the Arts.

SUZANNE LUMMIS was a 2018/19 COLA (City of Los Angeles) fellow. Her poems have appeared in *Ploughshares*, *Hotel Amerika*, *The Antioch Review*, *The New Yorker* and other national publications. *Poetry.la* produces her YouTube series *They Write by Night*, which draws together poetry and film noir and, occasionally, related political events. She's series editor of The Pacific Coast Poetry Series, an imprint of Beyond Baroque Books, and edited *Wide Awake Poets of Los Angeles and Beyond*, which then book editor of *The Los Angeles Times* David Ulin included in Ten Best Books of 2015.

JOY MANESIOTIS is the author of *They Sing to Her Bones*, which won the New Issues Poetry Prize. Her poems and essays have appeared in numerous literary journals, as well as in translation. Recently, she has staged *A Short History of Anger: A Hybrid Work of Poetry & Theatre*—a hybrid book-length manuscript with a Speaker and Greek Chorus—at festivals and universities in the U.S. and Europe. She is the Edith R. White Distinguished Professor in Creative Writing at the University of Redlands, in California. More information at joymanesiotis.com.

HOLADAY MASON is the author of two chapbooks and five full-length collections—*Towards the Forest* and *Dissolve* (New Rivers Press); *The Red Bowl: A Fable in Poems* (Red Hen Press); *The "She" Series: A Venice Correspondence*, with Sarah Maclay (What Books Press); and *The Weaver's Body* (Tebot Bach). Nominated for three Pushcart Prizes, her work has appeared in *Hotel Amerika*, *Spillway*, *Solo*, *Pool*, *Poetry International*, *The Laurel Review*, and more. She is also a portrait and fine art photographer focusing on the beauty of aging and humans as a part of nature. On Instagram @holadaymasonphotography (website the same name). Po Biz at holadaymason.com.

ANDREW MERTON's journalism and essays have appeared in publications including *The New York Times Magazine*, *Esquire*, *Ms. Magazine*, *Glamour*, and *Boston Magazine*. His poetry has appeared in the *Alaska*

Quarterly Review, Bellevue Literary Review, The Rialto, Comstock Review, Asheville Poetry Review, Louisville Review, The American Journal of Nursing, and elsewhere. He is the author of three books of poetry: *Evidence that We Are Descended from Chairs,* with a foreword by Charles Simic (Accents Publishing, 2012), *Lost and Found* (Accents Publishing, 2016), and *Final Exam* (Accents Publishing, 2019). He is a professor emeritus of English at the University of New Hampshire.

E. ETHELBERT MILLER is a literary activist and author of two memoirs and several poetry collections. He hosts the WPFW morning radio show On the Margin with E. Ethelbert Miller and hosts and produces *The Scholars on UDC-TV* which received a 2020 Telly Award. Most recently, Miller received a grant from the D.C. Commission on the Arts and Humanities and a congressional award from Congressman Jamie Raskin in recognition of his literary activism. Miller has two forthcoming books: *When Your Wife Has Tommy John Surgery and Other Baseball Stories* and *the little book of e.*

ROD VAL MOORE is the author of the short story collection, *Igloo Among Palms,* winner of the Iowa Short Fiction Award in 1994. His first novel, *A History of Hands,* won the 2013 Juniper Prize for Fiction, and is published by the University of Massachusetts Press. It was listed by Entropy.com as one of the ten best novels of the first half of 2014. Moore's second novel, Brittle Star, published by L.A.'s What Books Press, was selected by Foreward Reviews as the best science fiction novel of the year, and later nominated for the 2015 International IMPAC Dublin Literary Award.

NILS PETERSON is Professor Emeritus at San Jose State University of English and Humanities. He has published science fiction, several chapbooks, a memoir, and three collections of poetry. The last, *All the Marvelous Stuff,* was chosen as the best poetry book of the 2020 San Francisco Book Festival. In 2009, he was chosen to be the first Poet Laureate of Santa Clara County. Coleman Barks describes his poetry as "intelligent, lonely, funny and real. Necessary...."

ALEIDA RODRIGUEZ, Cuban-born poet, essayist, editor, was founder/ publisher of the first literary magazine and press by a woman/Latina/ lesbian in Los Angeles history (rara avis/Books of a Feather, 1977–84). Her debut collection, *Garden of Exile*, won the Kathryn A. Morton Poetry Prize, the PEN Literary Award, and was chosen a San Francisco Chronicle Best Book. She has received awards (NEA, COLA) and published in more than a hundred journals and anthologies nationally and internationally since 1974. From historic Red Hill House she teaches writing and consults on manuscripts. Two full-length collections—poetry, essays—are completed, with two chapbooks under construction.

MARTHA RONK is the author of eleven books of poetry, an ironic memoir, and a book of short stories. Her book, *Transfer of Qualities*, was long-listed for the National Book Award, Vertigo was a National Poetry Series selection, and *in a landscape of having to repeat* was a PEN USA best book of the year. Her work has been included in Wesleyan's anthology, *North American Poets in the 21st Century*. Her most recent is *Silences*, Omnidawn Press (2018), and she has three poetry books forthcoming.

CHUCK ROSENTHAL is the author of twelve novels, among them *The Loop Trilogy*; *Elena of the Stars*; *My Mistress, Humanity*; *The Heart of Mars*; *Ten Thousand Heavens*; *The Legend of La Diosa*; *The Hammer, the Sickle and the Heart* (2020). Rosenthal has published a memoir of childhood molestation, *Never Let Me Go*; a travel book, *Are We Not There Yet? Travels in Nepal, North India, and Bhutan*; a book of narrative essays, *West of Eden: A Life in 21st Century Los Angeles*; and two books of experimental poetry with Gail Wronsky. His book on animal cognition, *How the Animals Around You Think*, was published in October 2019.

SHARMAN APT RUSSELL is the author of a dozen books translated into nine languages. Her *Diary of a Citizen Scientist* won the 2016 John Burroughs Medal for Distinguished Nature Writing. Her *Within Our Grasp: Childhood Malnutrition Worldwide and the Revolution Taking Place to End It* (Pantheon Books, 2021) combines her longtime interest in hunger and in the environment. Recent fiction includes the award-winning eco-sci-fi *Knocking on Heaven's Door* and the YA *Teresa of the New World*. Sharman teaches in the low-residency MFA program at Antioch University in Los Angeles and lives in the magical realism of the American Southwest.

DIANE SEUSS's most recent collection is *frank: sonnets* (Graywolf Press, 2021). *Still Life with Two Dead Peacocks and a Girl*, (Graywolf Press, 2018) was a finalist for the National Book Critics Circle Award and *The Los Angeles Times* Book Prize in Poetry. *Four-Legged Girl* (Graywolf Press, 2015) was a finalist for the Pulitzer Prize. Seuss is a 2020 Guggenheim Fellow. She was raised by a single mother in rural Michigan, which she continues to call home.

GARY SOTO is the author of thirteen poetry collections for adults, most notably *New and Selected Poems*, a 1995 finalist for both *The Los Angeles Times* Award and the National Book Award. He has written several plays, including *In and Out of Shadows*, a musical about undocumented youth, and *The Afterlife*, a one-act play about teen murder and teen suicide. His most recent prose collection is *Sit Still! A Poet's Need to See and Do Everything*. He lives in Berkeley, California.

BONNIE SUMMERS, solidly over 60, is a mother and grandmother, social worker, advocate, gardener and a fan of jigsaw puzzles. Lucky enough to have been raised in the wide-open spaces of Wyoming and California's Central Valley, she now makes the Chicago area her home. *After Hours—A Journal of Chicago Writing and Art* published her first poem. She received the 2006 Guild Complex Prose Series Award for Nonfiction, Chicago, Illinois, and a Fall 2004 Money for Women, Barbara Deming Memorial Fund Award for Nonfiction. She continues to rely on her own and others' visual and written expressions to stay sane, aware and content. She wants to live all of her life.

SUSAN TERRIS's recent books are *Familiar Tense* (Marsh Hawk), 2019; *Take Two: Film Studies* (Omnidawn, 2017), *Memos* (Omnidawn, 2015); and *Ghost of Yesterday: New & Selected Poems* (Marsh Hawk, 2012). She's the author of seven books of poetry, seventeen chapbooks, three artist's books, and one play. Journals include *The Southern Review, Georgia Review, Prairie Schooner*, and *Ploughshares*. A poem of hers appeared in *Pushcart Prize XXXI*. A poem from *Memos* was in *Best American Poetry* (2015). Her newest book is *Dream Fragments*, which won the 2019 Swan Scythe Press Award. www.susanterris.com.

MELANIE RAE THON is a recipient of a Fellowship in Creative Arts from The John Simon Guggenheim Memorial Foundation, a Whiting Writer's Award, and two Fellowships from the National Endowment for the Arts. Her most recent books are *Silence & Song* (2015); *The 7th Man* (2015); and *The Bodies of Birds* (2019). As a teacher, explorer, and writer, she is devoted to the celebration of diversity from a multitude of human and more-than-human perspectives, shattering traditional limits of narrative consciousness as she interrogates the repercussions of exile, slavery, habitat loss, genocide, and extirpation in the context of mystery and miracle, the infinite wonder of cosmic abundance.

MICHAEL VENTURA is a writer. He and his wife now live near a lighthouse.

ELYCE WAKERMAN is the author of the novel, *A Tale of Two Citizens*, and two works of non-fiction: *Father Loss: Daughters Discuss the Man That Got Away* and *Air Powered: The Art of the Airbrush*. Her essays and articles have appeared in *The Los Angeles Times*, *The Jewish Journal*, and numerous magazines. Her TV credits include "Webster," "What's Happening Now?", and "Safe at Home." Elyce taught writing at California State University, Northridge from 1999 to 2012. She lives in Sherman Oaks with her husband, filmmaker Jeff Werner, and is writing a screenplay about a mother-daughter relationship, *Is That What You're Wearing?*

GARY YOUNG's most recent books are *That's What I Thought*, winner of the Lexi Rudnitsky Editor's Choice Award from Persea Books, and *Precious Mirror*, translations from the Japanese. His books include *Even So: New and Selected Poems*; *Pleasure*; *No Other Life*, winner of the William Carlos Williams Award; *Braver Deeds*, winner of the Peregrine Smith Poetry Prize; *The Dream of a Moral Life*, which won the James D. Phelan Award; and *Hands*. He has received grants from the NEH, NEA, and the Shelley Memorial Award from the Poetry Society of America among others. He teaches creative writing and directs the Cowell Press at UC Santa Cruz.

WHAT

BOOKS

PRESS

LOS ANGELES